MEET THE U.S.
People and Places
in the United States

Leslie Kagan
Boston University

Kay Westerfield
University of Oregon

Hoyong Park

Prentice Hall Regents, Englewood Cliffs, NJ 07632

Library of Congress Cataloging in Publication Data

KAGAN, LESLIE.
  Meet the U.S.

  1. English language—Text-books for foreign speakers.
  2. Readers—United States. 3. United States—Description
and travel—1980-   I. Westerfield, Kay.
II. Title.
PE1128.K27 1984   428.6′4   83-9504
ISBN 0-13-573808-3

Our thanks to Monte and Amelia,
André, Alexandra and Eliot,
and, of course, Steve.

Editorial production, supervision,
  and interior design by Lisa A. Domínguez
Cover design by Ray Lundgren
Cover drawing by Corinne Abbazia Hekker
Illustrations by Corinne Abbazia Hekker and Andrea Albahae
Manufacturing buyer: Harry P. Baisley

©1984 by Prentice Hall Regents
Prentice-Hall, Inc.
A Simon & Schuster Company
Englewood Cliffs, New Jersey 07632

Printed in the United States of America
20 19 18 17 16 15 14 13 12 11

ISBN 0-13-573808-3

Prentice-Hall International (UK) Limited, *London*
Prentice-Hall of Australia Pty. Limited, *Sydney*
Prentice-Hall Canada Inc., *Toronto*
Prentice-Hall Hispanoamericana, S.A., *Mexico*
Prentice-Hall of India Private Limited, *New Delhi*
Prentice-Hall of Japan, Inc., *Tokyo*
Simon & Schuster Asia Pte. Ltd., *Singapore*
Editora Prentice-Hall do Brasil, Ltda., *Rio de Janeiro*

Contents

Preface

For the Student

Meet the U.S. offers you the opportunity to improve your vocabulary and reading skills while increasing your knowledge of the culture and geography of the United States. Travel with reporter Lisa Evans as she drives across the United States writing articles for *The Boston Daily* newspaper, and become acquainted with the people and places she visits from Bangor, Maine to Honolulu, Hawaii. Meet the U.S.!

For the Teacher

Meet the U.S. is designed to develop the reading skills of ESL/EFL students at intermediate and advanced levels. The text touches upon many of the cultural and geographical variations that exist from region to region in the United States. *Meet the U.S.* develops an overall awareness of the United States, from its geography and its people to current issues and problems now facing the country. In regard to supplementary materials, the students' learning and enjoyment will be enhanced greatly by including some of the sights and sounds of each region; for example, a recording of bluegrass music for the Southeast or books with pictures of the national parks for the Mountain States will add another dimension to the class.

Highlights of Each Chapter

A. Take a Look This activity revolves around a regional map that shows state capitals, major cities, national parks, points of interest, and major industries. There are two sets of map exercises provided, one requiring short answers and the other requiring student-formulated questions based upon given information. For a change of pace, these exercises can be used as group games.

B. A Letter from Lisa   Lisa gives a friendly, interesting account of the area that she is visiting. Her letters include subjective comments on the scenery and reflections on local lifestyles, as well as personal anecdotes. Her letters also provide the student with examples of informal written language and offer a wide variety of colorful idiomatic expressions.

C. True or False?   This exercise serves as a quick comprehension check relating directly to the letter. To make the exercise more difficult, the students can be asked to correct the false statements.

D. Close-up   The focus of this cloze exercise alternates between determiners (odd-numbered chapters) and prepositions (even-numbered chapters). While the subject matter of this exercise is based upon the letter, the sentences are not taken directly from the text, thus making the exercise more challenging. A review of determiners may be helpful before doing the exercise.

E. Expressions   This is a vocabulary exercise in which the student must rewrite sentences, replacing certain words and phrases with appropriate new vocabulary taken from the letter. Since no definitions for the vocabulary items are provided, the sentences are carefully worded so that the meaning of the italiziced word(s) is clear from context.

F. Express Yourself   This exercise provides the students with the opportunity to use the new vocabulary items in different contexts, often directly related to the students' own experiences and opinions. This exercise can be used for oral and written practice.

G. Think Back   These comprehension questions on the letter require longer answers by the students. The exercise is suited for both oral and written work.

H. Talk About It   The students are given the opportunity to improve their speaking skills by talking about some of the issues presented in the letter and relating them to their own lives. These questions can also serve as topics for short compositions.

I. Words, Words, Words!   Each important new vocabulary item in the article is presented in a sentence illustrating its use. The students are challenged to figure out the meaning of the vocabulary word from the context of the sentence. When they have finished, the students can turn to the vocabulary list at the back of the book to check their definitions. The exercise is designed to make the students less dependent upon a dictionary by increasing their ability to use contextual clues. For variation, the students can work together in pairs or threes. At the teacher's option, this exercise can follow the reading of the article.

J. Headline   Each article presents a topic which is of both regional and national interest. We have carefully chosen subjects of both current and future relevance. In sharp contrast to the letter, the article is written in a more formal, journalistic style.

K. First Impressions   This multiple-choice exercise serves as a quick comprehension check relating directly to the article. After completing the exercise, the students can be asked to find the passage in the article that supports the correct answer.

L. Rapid Reading   In this exercise, which can be timed, the students develop their reading speed by scanning the article quickly for certain pieces of information. At the teacher's option, this exercise can precede the reading of the article.

M. Between the Lines   In this multiple-choice exercise the students develop their ability to read more discerningly, that is, "between the lines." The questions require the students to detect both main ideas and supporting examples, to be aware of implications, to guess the meaning of vocabulary items from context, and to understand specific pronoun references.

N. More Expressions   This is a vocabulary exercise in which the students complete sentences by choosing the appropriate item. In contrast to the sentences in vocabulary exercise *E,* the sentences provide fewer contextual clues for the answers as definitions for the vocabulary have already been given.

O. Express Yourself   See the description of exercise *F*.

P. Talk It Up   This exercise is a combination of exercises *G* and *H*. The first questions refer directly to the text; the remainder serve to stimulate class discussion about the article and related issues. Again, these questions can be used as topics for short compositions.

Q. Word Families   In doing these exercises the students are able to expand their vocabulary while increasing their knowledge of the different parts of speech—noun, verb, adjective, and adverb. The students are asked to complete interesting sentences with the correct word form, paying attention to both verb tense and voice, and singular or plural form of the noun. At least one member of each word family has been used in either the letter or the article.

R. Look It Up   This exercise encourages students to use the library and other sources of reference outside the classroom. In this manner, the students themselves provide additional information about the region, while improving their library skills. This exercise lends itself nicely to both individual and group work, and the questions may serve as topics for compositions or short oral reports.

Prologue

...and then Steve called me into his office and asked me if I'd be interested in writing my own series of articles for *The Boston Daily* on the different regions of the United States. "Interested?" I said, "I'd be delighted! When do I start?"

Anyway, to make a long story short, I'll be traveling for about three months. I decided to drive rather than fly as that way I can see more of the country and have a more flexible schedule. My Chevy should be O.K. for the trip, and if I have any car problems, my travel expenses should pay for them.

Yes, Steve and I have become close friends over the past couple of years. I admire and respect him as an editor; he's really helped me develop my own journalistic style. Thanks to him, I think I've turned into a pretty good newspaper reporter.

I'm glad you decided to go to school in Boston this summer, so you can "apartment-sit" for me while I'm gone. I'll leave detailed instructions for watering the plants, feeding the cat, and the like. Thanks a lot.

Love,

Lisa

MEET THE U.S.

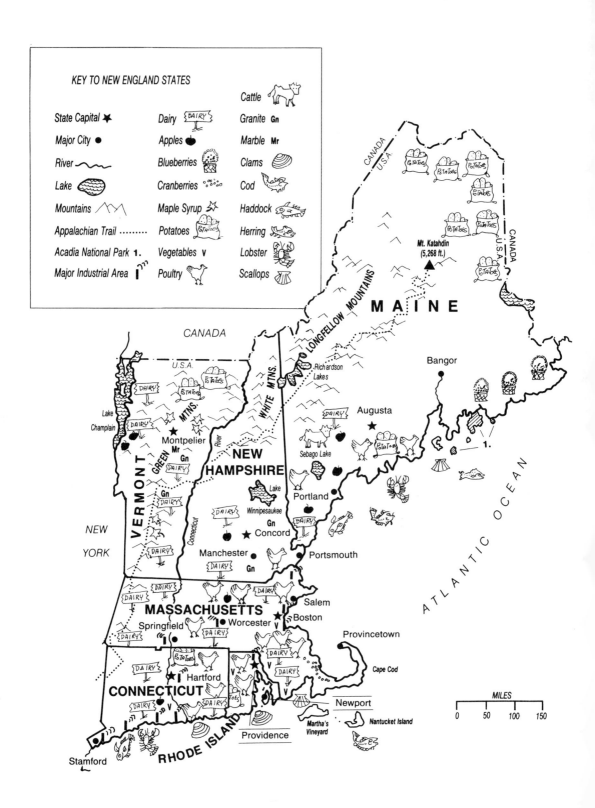

chapter 1

New England

con-né d-i-cut

A. Take a Look

I. Answer the following questions by looking at the map:

1. What is the capital of the largest state in New England?
2. Which two states have the Connecticut River as a border?
3. How many states touch the Atlantic Ocean?
4. In which state is Hartford?
5. Which state in New England grows the most potatoes?
6. Which states border on New York state?

Maine state
Maine

II. Make up questions that could be answered by the following information:

1. Acadia National Park
2. Boston
3. 5,268 feet
4. Martha's Vineyard and Nantucket
5. At the northern tip of Cape Cod

B. A Letter from Lisa

Bangor, Maine
June 4

Dear Steve,

Well, Mr. Editor, my first article, "There's Nothing Like a Diner," is typed and in the mail to you. One down and nine to go. It still doesn't seem real—traveling around the U.S.A. and writing my own series of articles on contemporary America. It's a journalist's dream come true!

Here I am, though, in Bangor, Maine, lying on my hotel bed and trying to calm my upset stomach. I've literally been eating my way up the coast of New England. Maybe I should be writing a gourmet food column instead of the articles. Today, for example, I had pancakes with fresh blueberries and maple syrup for breakfast, sweet corn and steamers[1] for lunch, and of course, boiled lobster with melted butter for dinner. Maine seafood is a real treat. Did you know it takes lobsters seven years to grow one pound? It's no surprise they're so delicious—and expensive!

I couldn't believe it when you told me you'd never been to Maine. Having grown up here, I may be partial, but I really think it's a great place to be—winter, spring, summer, or fall. Each season is special in its own way, but fall is definitely my favorite. The air is crisp, the days are cool, and the leaves on the trees turn the most incredibly vivid shades of red, yellow, and orange, almost as if they had been set on fire. People come from all over the United States just to see the fall foliage,[2] and it's well worth the long trip. Of course, as early as October it starts to get cold and the colors fade. The wind and the rain strip the last leaves from the trees, and it's time for winter.

Winters here are unbearable if you don't like snow, but if you like winter sports, as most people around here do, Maine's a winter wonderland. Even now in the summer, I see a lot of cars with out-of-season "Think Snow" bumper stickers.[3] This past year, most of the snow was gone by the end of March, and the frustrated skiers are still grumbling about the dry winter.

Actually, Maine has five seasons, or so the natives say. After winter comes "mud season," which is an appropriate description of the month of April in Maine. Rising temperatures melt the snow and turn the frozen ground into mud. Even worse, as the ice and snow disappear, so do big chunks of road. I saw a pothole[4] yesterday that was big enough to take a bath in! Well, maybe I am exaggerating just a little, but by the time the road crews fill in all the holes, it'll probably be winter again! By the way, will my business expenses pay for new shock absorbers[5] for the car?

Eventually spring does come to Maine. Almost overnight the "closed for the winter" signs are taken off the doors of the innumerable tourist traps, including the ever popular antique shops, the moccasin and deerskin glove trading posts[6] and the fast-food stands. By June, it seems as if half the front lawns in Maine are littered with yard sale[7] items—outgrown baby highchairs, vacuum cleaners with broken plugs, last winter's snow tires, and the like. You can get some real bargains! As the old saying goes, "Your trash may be someone else's treasure!"

Of course, most tourists visit Maine in the summer. Those who come expecting to swim in warm water are disappointed, if not horrified, when they try the Atlantic Ocean in Maine. The water temperature hardly ever goes above 65°. The trick to swimming in Maine is to get your feet wet and wait until they're too numb to feel the cold. Then you can swim, and you don't feel a thing!

That's Maine, the state of the five seasons. You get a real sense of the life cycle of nature when you spend a year here. It's also fitting to begin my journey in the first state to see the sun rise in the morning.

Tomorrow I head south for the Big Apple[8]—New York, New York! I won't have time to stop in Boston, so please say hello to everyone at the Daily for me.

Love,

Lisa

P.S. Did you know that one lobster claw is always bigger than the other? Like humans, lobsters are either left- or right-handed, or is it "clawed"?

Notes

1. steamers: steamed clams.
2. foliage: the leaves of trees and plants.
3. bumper sticker: a strip of paper with a message printed on it that is placed on the bumper of a car.
4. pothole: a pot-shaped hole in a road surface.
5. shock absorbers: the part of a car used to absorb the bumps in a road and make the ride smoother.
6. moccasin and deerskin glove trading posts: small shops featuring local souvenirs, especially moccasins and deerskin gloves.
7. yard sale: an outdoor sale where used personal items of one or more families are sold at inexpensive prices.
8. Big Apple: a slang expression for New York City.

C. True or False?

Write T before those statements that are true and F before those that are false.

_____ 1. A three-pound lobster is probably 21 years old.
_____ 2. Although she had grown up in Boston, Lisa had spent a lot of time in Maine.

_____ 3. Lisa thinks that it's almost impossible to fill in all the potholes between winters.

_____ 4. At a yard sale you can find items that the owner no longer wants, but that you may need.

_____ 5. Too much traveling gave Lisa an upset stomach.

_____ 6. Mud is a mixture of water and dirt.

_____ 7. Many of Maine's businesses are seasonal.

_____ 8. Lisa thinks that it's fitting to begin her trip through the United States in Maine because that's where she was born.

_____ 9. Even in the summer, the water of the Atlantic Ocean off Maine is extremely cold.

_____ 10. In a dry winter there's a lot of snow but little rain.

D. Close-up

Fill in the blanks with a, an, or the. If no article is necessary, put an X in the blank.

Fishing has been _____ established industry in _____ Maine for more
              (1)   (2)

than 400 years. Today Rockland is _____ leading fishing port in _____
                               (3)   (4)

state. Each August, _____ city celebrates its industry with _____
                       (5)   (6)

Maine Seafoods Festival. _____ tourists come from near and far to
                             (7)

sample _____ lobsters, _____ clams and other delicious seafoods.
         (8)   (9)

After all, _____ visit to _____ state of Maine would be incomplete
          (10)   (11)

without _____ seafood dinner. As any Maine native would tell you,
        (12)

_____ Maine seafood is _____ best in _____ world!
(13)   (14)   (15)

E. Expressions

Rewrite the following sentences, replacing the italicized words with the correct form of the appropriate word or expression.

unbearable	partial (to)	vivid
fitting	innumerable	chunk
littering	to grumble	numb
	to fade	

1. Car license plates in Maine say "Maine—vacationland," an *appropriate* title for a state in which tourism is a major industry.

2. Every spring, Elmer Smith carefully repaints the sign above his corner market, and every winter, the rain and snow do their work, and once again, the letters *lose their colors*.

3. Skiers at Killington, Vermont have to wear warm gloves and socks so that their fingers and toes don't become *devoid of sensation* in the below-freezing temperatures.   sensation – sense, feeling
   devoid – Not有, 거의없 죽은

4. Highways in New England are very clean, probably because people have to pay a heavy fine for *throwing trash away improperly*.

5. Although tourism is important to New England's economy, many natives resent the yearly invasion of vacationers and can be heard *muttering in discontent,* "those darn tourists!"   resent – feel angry at

6. Before electric refrigerators were invented, people cut *big pieces* of ice out of frozen lakes every winter and buried them until the summer when they were used to keep food cool.   cloud – 먹이

7. During the month of June, clouds of black flies make the woods in New England *intolerable* for campers.

8. The state of New Hampshire, with its mountains and beaches, offers *countless* ways to spend a delightful summer vacation.

9. Although Lisa thinks the sandy beaches of Cape Cod, Massachusetts are beautiful, she is *more fond of* the rocky coast of Maine.

10. Lisa's visit to Maine brought back *sharp* memories of her childhood.

F. Express Yourself

1. In a trial of justice, it is important that members of the jury be *impartial* (the opposite of *partial*). Why? Do you think this is possible? Why or why not?

criminal case – 12

criminal
the state – who prosecute? – civil other one.   wrongful death.

2. The word *fade* is used in many different contexts. What does it mean in the following examples, and what has caused the *fading?*
    a. *faded* blue jeans
    b. the flowered curtains were *faded*
    c. a *faded* photograph
    d. the music *faded*
    e. a *faded* memory

3. Are there fines for *littering* in your native country? Some people claim that biodegradable items, such as apple cores and banana peels, are not *litter*. Do you agree?

G. Think Back

Answer the following questions according to the text.

1. What is Lisa's profession and current project?

2. Why do native Mainers say that the state has five seasons?

3. Why does Lisa need new shock absorbers for her car?

4. If you needed a lamp, but didn't have the money to buy a new one, where could you look for one?

5. Which season does Lisa prefer and why?

H. Talk About It

1. Which season would you prefer in Maine and why?

2. In your native country, what kind of food is your region famous for?

3. Think of everything you have but don't use in your room, apartment, or house and make a list of possible yard sale items. You may even want to have a yard sale in class or school.

I. Words, Words, Words!

The following vocabulary items have been taken from Lisa's article. Try to guess the meaning of each word from the context and write your definition in the space provided. When you have finished, check the vocabulary list at the end of the book for the correct meaning.

1. ban _____
   Massachusetts law *bans* the sale of alcoholic beverages in stores on Sunday. Residents have to wait until Monday to buy liquor.

2. dilapidated _____

The old covered bridge in rural New Hampshire was so *dilapidated* that it had to be closed.

3. duplicate _____

It is impossible for manufacturers to *duplicate* the taste of pure maple syrup; there is simply nothing else like it.

4. enterprising _____

Over the past two decades, *enterprising* businessmen have taken over sleepy ski areas throughout New England and turned them into large, profitable ski resorts.

5. extinction _____

Unrestricted hunting resulted in the near *extinction* of the wild turkey, a bird which was once very common in the forests of New England.

6. gossip _____

In small towns, everyone knows everyone else's business because *gossip* is a favorite pastime.

7. layout _____

The *layout* of early New England towns always included a community grazing area, called a Common, in the center.

8. linger _____

Visitors to the island of Nantucket off the coast of Cape Cod would rather *linger* on the beautiful island than hurry back to the mainland.

9. merely _____

Since Boston is *merely* 45 minutes by plane from New York, many business executives fly daily between the two cities.

10. nickname _____

"Old Ironsides" is the *nickname* for Boston's *U.S.S. Constitution,* a 1797 warship whose wooden sides were as strong as iron.

11. proponent _____

Proponents of the movement to clean up America's lakes, rivers, and streams are delighted by the progress made in Maine.

12. replica _____

At the maritime museum in Mystic, Connecticut, visitors can buy miniature *replicas* of whaling ships from the 19th century.

13. substantial _____

New Hampshire is known as the "Granite State" because it provides a *substantial* amount of the world's granite.

An ideal spot for a late night snack.

J. Headline

THERE'S NOTHING LIKE A DINER

by Lisa Evans

1   They are scattered along the major roads throughout the Northeast. From the parking lots, they look like railroad or trolley cars, but the cheery curtains in the windows, the flower boxes on the window sills, and the "Come on in, we're open" signs on the doors suggest something different. These are the diners, where eating is a unique restaurant experience.

2   The first diners appeared almost one hundred years ago. Originally they were horse-drawn wagons filled with sandwiches, hot dogs, desserts, and coffee for people who wanted to eat out after 8:00 P.M. Many restaurants were already closed by that hour, but the diner stayed open, thus earning the nickname, "night owl." As these "night owls" gradually grew in popularity, their equipment and decor became more sophisticated and their menu more substantial.

3   It was not until 1897, though, that the trolley design of the diner became popular. When Boston, Philadelphia, and New York City replaced their horse-drawn trolleys with modern electric cars, the abandoned models were bought by enterprising merchants for 15 or 20 dollars and turned into diners. It was also during this period, however, that the diners suffered a loss of respectability. The dilapidated cars tended to drive away respectable customers while attracting a less desirable clientele. At one point in their history, diners were even banned by city order in Atlantic City, New Jersey and Buffalo, New York.

4   Fortunately the diners were saved from possible extinction by a man named Patrick

(Pop) Tierny, who, in the early 1900s, created a more elegant version of the old trolley diner. Inspired by the railroad dining car, "Pop" added booths,[1] small windows, and a barrel roof to his diners. During this same period, automobiles were growing in popularity and long distance travel was becoming more common. Diners along the roadside provided both pleasant and convenient stopping places for hungry travelers. Thanks to Tierny's changes in decor and to the increased number of cars on the roads, the diners were back in business.

5   During the first half of the twentieth century, the diner manufacturing industry came into being and grew at the same rapid pace as the American[2] highway system. The authentic diner (to be distinguished from the numerous tiny restaurants that call themselves diners) was an entirely prefabricated,[3] movable replica of a turn-of-the-century trolley or railroad car. The diner could be easily transported to wherever seemed to be a well-traveled spot.

6   To imply that the diner is merely a restaurant is misleading. In fact, the diner is a miniature "community" centered around a grillman. Unlike most restaurants that hide the kitchen in the back, the diner places the grill out front, in clear view.. Cooking becomes a public performance to which all customers are invited. The grillman knows how to crack both jokes and eggs and is often as good at making up stories as he is at making a meal. A talent for public relations as well as a talent for cooking are required for his job.

7   The layout of the diner also encourages this communal spirit. The regular customers sit facing the grillman on slippery stools that are bolted[4] to the floor at a sometimes uncomfortable distance from the counter; short customers have to lean forward to reach their food. The "regulars" come from all walks of life; lawyers and policemen sit elbow to elbow with bankers and trashmen. They share the local gossip and occasionally the same coffee spoon. Families and groups of friends, on the other hand, tend to gather in the well-padded booths for more private conversation and dining. There is, however, a lot of conversational interaction between those on the stools and those in the booths.

8   Diners are often run by families. Dad may do the cooking and Mom the waitressing, while the kids help out wherever needed. The service is "homestyle" and usually fast, although customers are welcome to linger all morning over a cup of coffee with several refills.

9   Good home cooking is another basic tradition of the diner. Glass cases display rows upon rows of pies covered with whipped cream, and rich chocolate layer cakes, all homemade by caring hands. The menu, usually hanging above the grill, features such American mainstays[5] as meatloaf, grilled cheese, tuna fish, and, of course, hamburgers and hot dogs. The portions are generous and the prices are low.

10   Not so long ago there were many diners to provide quick, inexpensive meals in an informal setting. Today innumerable fast-food chains[6] with carbohydrate-filled menus and billion-dollar advertising budgets aimed at capturing the American on the run also offer quick, inexpensive meals in an informal atmosphere. Where does the diner fit in? It cannot even try to compete on such a grand scale and, unfortunately, many have closed their doors. Actually, in the eyes of its proponents, the diner does not have to compete; it has a spirit which cannot be duplicated. So, the next time you are on the road and ready for a bite to eat, try a diner.

Notes

1. booth: a table in a restaurant with two backed benches.
2. American: Although technically "American" refers to all of North, South, and Central America, in the United States it is more commonly used to refer to someone or something from the U.S.
3. prefabricated: a term referring to a structure whose standardized parts have already been partially assembled in the factory.
4. bolted: attached permanently.
5. mainstay: a typical food.
6. fast-food chain: a group of restaurants, such as McDonald's, with the same name, menu, and decor.

K. First Impressions

Do the following exercise without referring to the article. Circle the letter next to the statement that best answers the question.

1. Throughout the article, the term "diner" refers to
   a. an evening meal.
   b. a person eating in a restaurant.
   c. a type of restaurant.
   d. a horse-drawn wagon.

2. In the beginning the diner's customers were primarily
   a. businessmen during their lunch hour.
   b. people who wanted a late meal.
   c. travelers.
   d. families.

3. According to the article, what saved the diner from extinction?
   a. Improvements in the diner's interior decor.
   b. An increase in the number of people traveling by car.
   c. A decrease in the number of people traveling by train.
   d. Both a and b.
   e. All of the above.

4. Lisa compares the growth of the diner manufacturing industry to the growth of
   a. the highway system.
   b. the railroad.
   c. the fast-food industry.
   d. the trolley system.

5. Which of the following statements is false?
   a. The diner has always had the trolley design.
   b. The diner has two types of seating arrangements.
   c. Lisa feels that the diner is more than just a restaurant.
   d. The food in the diner can best be described as "good home cooking."

L. Rapid Reading

Do this exercise in class. Scan the article quickly to find the following pieces of information. Write down the number of the paragraph in which each topic is discussed.

a. _____ the regulars

b. _____ the "night owl"

c. _____ introduction of the trolley design

d. _____ fast-food chains

e. _____ "Pop" Tierny's improvements

f. _____ American mainstays

g. _____ the diner manufacturing industry

h. _____ the family service

i. _____ a miniature community

M. Between the Lines

Circle the letter next to the statement that best answers the question. You may refer to the text.

1. The main idea of the article is
   a. the design of the diner.
   b. the creation of the fast-food chain.
   c. American eating habits.
   d. the history of the diner.

2. The diner "regulars" are
   a. lawyers and policemen.
   b. bankers and trashmen.
   c. travelers.
   d. people from all professions.

3. The "American on the run" in paragraph 10 refers to
   a. a jogger.
   b. an escapee from prison.
   c. a very busy person.
   d. a traveling American.

4. In paragraph 4, sentence 3, "this same period" refers to
   a. the first half of the nineteenth century.
   b. 1897.
   c. the early 1900s.
   d. the late 1800s.

5. Paragraph 10 implies that
   a. competition from big business has hurt the diner.
   b. the diner is competing successfully with large fast-food restaurants.
   c. the number of diners has increased in recent years.
   d. the diner has lost business because the service is too slow and the prices are too high.

N. More Expressions

Fill in the blanks with words from the following list. Use the correct voice, tense, and singular or plural form of the noun.

to ban	nickname	substantial
dilapidated	to linger	replica
to duplicate	merely	enterprising
	proponent	

1. The _____ buildings along the waterfront in New Haven were torn down to make room for new apartment buildings.

2. P. T. Barnum, a(n) _____ resident of Bridgeport, Connecticut, started a circus which soon became known as "The Greatest Show on Earth."

3. _____ of public transportation feel that the passenger trains on the East Coast should receive more support from the federal government.

4. "Bean Town" is the _____ for Boston, a city famous for its baked beans.

5. Littering _____ by law throughout the United States.

6. The seasick passenger on the ferry between Providence and Block Island regretted having eaten such a _____ breakfast.

7. Lisa _____ the key to her apartment and gave the copy to her nextdoor neighbor.

8. The art student _____ in Boston's Museum of Fine Arts long after her friends had left.

9. Farmhouses in Maine are not _____ attractive; being attached to the barns, they are also extremely practical in the cold winter months.

10. The John Hancock Building in downtown Boston houses a(n)

_____ of eighteenth century Boston complete with lights, music, and an informative recorded text.

O. Express Yourself

1. Do you have a *nickname?* If so, how did you get it?

2. Which adjectives would describe an *enterprising* businessman? What do you think an "enterprise" is?

3. The prefix "pro-" in *proponent* means "in favor of"; for example, a *proponent* of nuclear energy is pronuclear and an opponent is antinuclear. What are some other current issues a person can be for (pro-) or against (anti-)?

P. Talk It Up

1. Why were diners called "night owls"?

2. What distinguishes a diner from a fast-food chain restaurant?

3. Does your native country have chain restaurants?

4. What are some of the common "fast foods" in your native country?

Q. Word Families

Choose the appropriate form of the word. Be certain to use the correct verb tense, singular or plural form of the noun, and the passive voice where necessary.

1. frustration, to frustrate, frustrating, frustrated
   a. Taking the subway in Boston can be a _____ experience.
   b. _____ passengers sometimes have to wait as much as half an hour for their trains.
   c. There is nothing worse than the _____ of waiting for the subway when you are already late for work.
   d. Finding a solution to the subway's problems _____ authorities for a long time.

2. exaggeration, to exaggerate, exaggerated
   a. It is no _____ to say that New Hampshire's lakes and streams are filled with big fish.

b. However, Joe White liked _____ the size of the fish he caught.

c. When no one believed his _____ story about catching a 15-pound trout, Joe replied, "You should have seen the one that got away!"

3. inspiration, to inspire, inspiring, inspired
   a. Many famous poets and writers found _____ for their work in the New England countryside.
   b. Benjamin Franklin was an _____ scientist, inventor, writer, and statesman.
   c. His writings _____ readers for over 200 years.
   d. Franklin's contributions had an _____ effect on eighteenth century society.

4. industry, to industrialize, industrial, industrious
   a. The coming of textile mills to Lowell, Massachusetts in the nineteenth century _____ the previously rural area.
   b. The textile and shoe _____ employ thousands of people in New England.
   c. Southern New England is one of the major _____ areas in the United States.
   d. An _____ student may receive a scholarship to one of New England's prestigious universities.

5. conversation, conversationalist, to converse, conversational
   a. After having corrected final exams all night, the E.S.L. instructor from Boston University did not feel very _____ when she boarded the plane for New York.
   b. Being so tired, she was disappointed to discover that she had been given a seat next to a man who was a _____.
   c. They _____ for a short time about the advantages of living in Boston.
   d. Finally no longer able to stay awake, the teacher suddenly ended the _____ with a loud snore.

6. comfort, to comfort, comfortable, comforting, comfortably
   a. In the state of New Hampshire there are many _____ old inns where travelers can stop for the night.
   b. Lisa dressed _____ for the long drive from Boston to Bangor.
   c. Knowing that she had a spare tire in the trunk of her car was a _____ thought to Lisa as she drove along the bumpy road.
   d. The mother _____ her crying child who had gotten lost in the museum.
   e. On cold, snowy, winter nights, people in New England can spend evenings in _____ sitting around a warm woodstove.

7. (in)appropriateness, (in)appropriate, (in)appropriately
   a. Backpackers in Vermont's Green Mountains have to dress _____ for hiking.
   b. Sandals, for example, are definitely _____ for the rough trails.
   c. The _____ of Rutland's nickname, the "Marble City," is clear when one considers the huge marble fields surrounding the Vermont resort center.

8. to distinguish, distinguishing, distinguished
   a. The numerous marine laboratories in Woods Hole, Massachusetts _____ the small town from others on Cape Cod.
   b. _____ scientists come from all over the world to do research at the various institutes.
   c. Another _____ feature of Woods Hole is the town's drawbridge, which raises to let boats into the harbor.

9. tradition, traditional, traditionally
   a. Thanksgiving is a _____ holiday in New England and in the rest of the United States.
   b. It is a _____ for families to get together and have a big dinner on this day.
   c. Cranberries, which are a major crop on Cape Cod, are _____ served with turkey for the holiday meal.

10. description, to describe, descriptive, descriptively
   a. Interested in buying a woodstove, the customer picked up a brochure which _____ various models of stoves made by the Vermont Castings Company.
   b. A _____ passage in the brochure gave the history of the New England company.
   c. The _____ of the woodstoves included instructions for cleaning them.
   d. The brochure also _____ illustrated the different models in a diagram.

R. Look It Up

1. What is a "litterbug"?

2. Who was Paul Revere and what was his famous cry?

3. What happened in Salem, Massachusetts in 1692 that made the town infamous?

4. Many old houses in New England fishing villages were built with widow's walks. What is a widow's walk and how do you think it got its name?

5. What happened at Plymouth Rock?

6. Can you answer the following New England riddle? If April showers bring May flowers, what do Mayflowers bring?

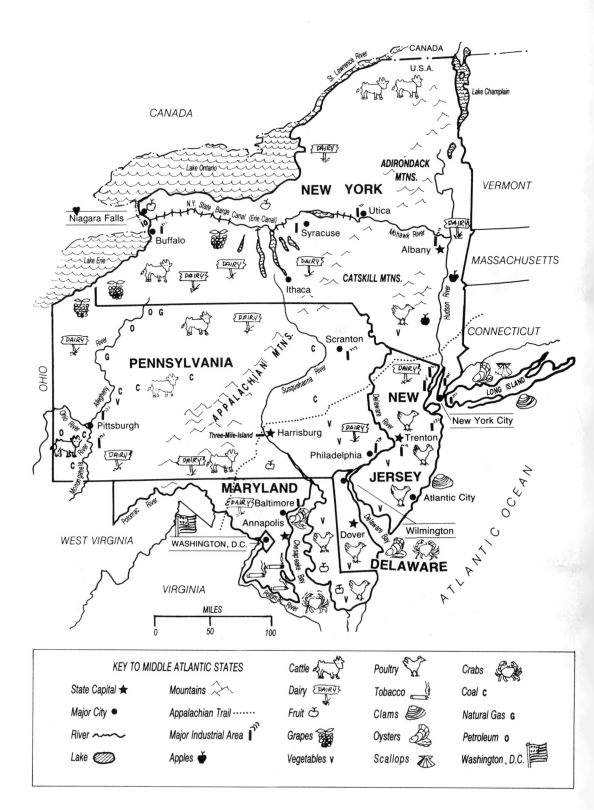

CANADA

St. Lawrence River

CANADA

U.S.A.

Lake Champlain

Lake Ontario

ADIRONDACK MTNS.

NEW YORK

VERMONT

Niagara Falls

N.Y. State Barge Canal (Erie Canal)

Buffalo

Lake Erie

Utica

DAIRY

Syracuse

Mohawk River

Albany

MASSACHUSETTS

DAIRY

DAIRY

DAIRY

Ithaca

CATSKILL MTNS.

Hudson River

CONNECTICUT

OHIO

O G

O

DAIRY

River

G

PENNSYLVANIA

C

DAIRY

APPALACHIAN MTNS.

Scranton

C

Susquehanna River

C

DAIRY

LONG ISLAND

Allegheny River

C

C

V

Ohio River

Pittsburgh

Three-Mile-Island

Harrisburg

Delaware River

NEW

New York City

DAIRY

V

DAIRY

Trenton

DAIRY

Monongahela River

C

C

DAIRY

Philadelphia

JERSEY

Atlantic City

MARYLAND

Potomac River

DAIRY Baltimore

Annapolis

Wilmington

WEST VIRGINIA

WASHINGTON, D.C.

Chesapeake Bay

V

Dover

Delaware Bay

DELAWARE

ATLANTIC OCEAN

VIRGINIA

Potomac River

V

MILES

0   50   100

chapter 2

The Middle Atlantic States

New York
Pennsylvania
New Jersey
Long Island
Delaware
Maryland
⋆ Washington DC.

A. Take a Look

I. Answer the following questions by looking at the map:

1. Which river forms the southern border of Maryland?
2. Which bodies of water form the border between New York and Canada?
3. What is another name for the New York State Barge Canal?
4. Which sources of energy can be found in Pennsylvania?
5. Which two mountain ranges are found in New York state?
6. What types of seafood are found off the coast of Long Island?

II. Make up questions that could be answered by the following information:

1. They meet in Pittsburgh.
2. Along Lake Erie and in western New York
3. On the Potomac River, between Maryland and Virginia
4. Dover
5. The western border of New Jersey

B. A Letter from Lisa

New York City
June 9

Dear Steve,

Sunday afternoon in Central Park[1]—there's nothing else quite like it. People of all ages, who didn't leave the city for the weekend, get together here for sun and fun. On one side of me, a boy and his dad are unsuccessfully trying to launch a Spiderman[2] kite on this hot, windless day. Off to the other side, there are hustlers[3] selling cans of beer for a buck.[4] By the fountain, there are a few dope[5] dealers, covertly offering illegal drugs to any interested passersby. I can see a man on six-foot stilts[6] who's getting a lot of attention and a group of folk dancers in bright costumes, stepping to lively music. To my right there's a saxophonist, and to my left a flutist is playing for pennies or pleasure, probably for both. There are also the sun worshipers trying to get a tan through the polluted haze hanging over the city. And everywhere there are joggers, bicyclists, and rollerskaters wearing headphones plugged into miniature cassette decks belted to their waists; they go racing by, oblivious to any noise other than the latest tune in their ears.

I've been staying with my sister who is an English teacher here. Rents are unbelievably high in Manhattan, so she lives in a studio apartment the size of a large closet. Her desk serves as a kitchen table, and the couch turns into her bed at night. I'm not sure I'd like to live like that, but she does have the city at her doorstep.

Although it's not difficult to find your way around downtown Manhattan, the traffic is terrible. To make matters worse, it's almost impossible to find parking on the street. I simply left my Chevy in a garage and have been using public transportation ever since.

Speaking of which, taking the subway here is a real experience. The interiors of the cars are decorated with all types of graffiti[7] from peace symbols to obscenities. Some of the exteriors have been artistically painted by vandals[8] and look like they belong in an amusement park rather than in a subway. Last night, I spotted two members of the Guardian Angels[9] with their red berets. I'd heard so much about them, it was exciting to see them. Nothing spectacular happened, though. They stayed on the train for a few stations checking with other Guardian Angels at each stop to see if all was well. The passengers seemed to be aware of them and were probably thankful for their presence, but my sister says they don't attract much attention anymore; people are used to them. Did I feel safer? I suppose I did.

I can imagine that living in this city could be difficult at times. The tiniest apartment costs a fortune to rent and has three or more locks on the front door and bars on the windows if it's on the ground floor. You get nervous if someone

bad
language

saw

has been walking behind you for more than a block. Bus drivers are without pity if you don't have the exact change, and impatient, rude cashiers are the rule rather than the exception.

On the other hand, New York City is incredibly dynamic. You can walk for hours past little newsstands, colorful flower stalls, and a multitude of sidewalk vendors, selling everything from folding umbrellas to warm, fat pretzels. You can [Grinits] shop at Macy's, the world's largest department store, or go to Greenwich Village[10] for cappuccino with whipped cream and cinnamon in a little café where paintings from the Italian Renaissance hang on the walls. You can view New York by night from the top of the World Trade Center, 100 flights up, or just stand down in the street and watch the continually changing messages on the huge neon sign in Times Square. You can catch a hit Broadway show, go to the ballet, or spend a quiet afternoon at the Museum of Modern Art, admiring such masterpieces as Monet's "Waterlilies."

Yesterday morning, my sister and I took a ride on the Battery Park Ferry out to the Statue of Liberty. I'd never been there before and was moved by the inscription[11] welcoming the poor and homeless of the world to the shores of the United States. It's so fitting, especially for a city like New York, where you can have your coat altered by a Chinese tailor, get a beer next door in an Irish pub, and finally purchase an expensive camera inexpensively in a store run by orthodox Jews. They're all here, immigrants from all over the world, living in a country where the term "Native American" refers only to the Indians. For the past 400 years, the tendency has been for them to conform; they have given up their languages and cultures in favor of English and the American way of life. I get the impression, though, that this is changing. Americans of all cultural groups are becoming more interested in preserving their own ethnic identity.

Hey! There goes the ice cream man! A vanilla cone is just what I need right now.

Bye,

Lisa

Notes

1. Central Park: an 840-acre park located in Manhattan, the center of New York City.
2. Spiderman: a cartoon character noted for his spider-like abilities that help him fight crime.
3. hustler: a person selling something with aggressive enthusiasm.
4. buck: (slang) dollar.
5. dope: (slang) illegal drugs.
6. stilts: poles that enable the user to walk several feet above the ground.
7. graffiti: writing on the walls, often including different slogans or obscenities (vulgar language).

taggers – people who draw graffiti.

8. vandal: a person who destroys public or private property.
9. Guardian Angels: a controversial group of concerned citizens that was created to fight crime and violence in New York City streets and especially subways.
10. Greenwich Village: a section of New York City famous for its liberal lifestyle and its jazz nightclubs.
11. last lines of the inscription on the Statue of Liberty:
    "Give me your tired, your poor, your huddled masses yearning to breathe free, the wretched refuse of your teeming shore. Send these, the homeless, tempest-tossed, to me! I lift my lamp beside the golden door."

C. True or False?

Write T before those statements that are true and F before those that are false.

_____ 1. Lisa's sister is living in a very small apartment because rents in downtown New York City are very high.

_____ 2. Lisa decided not to drive in New York City because she was afraid of getting lost.

_____ 3. The term "Native American" refers to the first English immigrants to the United States.

_____ 4. People who live in New York like to leave the city and spend the weekend in Central Park.

_____ 5. Buying and selling drugs in Central Park is permitted by law.

_____ 6. Lisa feels that many ethnic groups in the United States now want to preserve their heritage more than earlier generations did.

_____ 7. The World Trade Center is the largest department store in the world.

_____ 8. The Guardian Angels want New Yorkers to feel safer in the subway.

_____ 9. Lisa feels that New York City has both bad and good points.

_____ 10. New York City got some of its subway cars from an amusement park.

D. Close-up

Fill in the blanks with the appropriate prepositions.

Only about two hours _____ car and ferry _____ downtown Manhattan
                    (1)   (2)

lies Fire Island, a popular vacation spot _____ city-weary New Yorkers.
                                       (3)

Threatened _____ beach erosion and _____ its location close _____
         (4)   (5)   (6)

New York City, this beautiful island is now a national seashore _____
                                                                  (7)

the protection _____ the National Park Service. _____ the island, there
               (8)   (9)

are no roads _____ ordinary cars, and its small communities can be
             (10)

reached only _____ boat. A visitor _____ the island can still enjoy a
             (11)   (12)

peaceful walk _____ an almost deserted beach, and forget, if only
              (13)

_____ a short time, the huge skyscrapers and fast pace associated
 (14)

_____ city living.
 (15)

E. Expressions

Rewrite the following sentences, replacing the italicized words with the correct form of the appropriate word or expression.

to conform (to)	to launch	masterpiece
spectacular	worshiper	pity
to spot	oblivious (to)	multitude
	covertly	

1. The latest Broadway show was described as *sensational* by the normally reserved drama critic of the *New York Times.*

2. While walking down Fifth Avenue, Lisa had the good fortune *to notice* the actor, Woody Allen, in front of her, so she took the opportunity to ask him for his autograph.

3. Many New Yorkers consider the World Trade Center to be a *supreme achievement* of American architecture.

4. Taking advantage of the woman's purse being open, the thief *secretly* reached in and stole her wallet.

5. The saleswoman in Macy's carefully wrapped the package for the customer, *unconscious of* the fact that the customer was Pat Nixon, wife of former President Richard Nixon.

6. Most immigrants to the United States weren't looking for *sympathy;* they were looking for the opportunity to start a new life.

7. Every Fourth of July in New York City, hundreds of fireworks *are sent off* into the air where they explode into all sorts of shapes and colors.

8. The state of New York isn't only for those people who like city living. Nature *lovers* are very happy living in the beautiful Catskill Mountains of upper New York State.

9. A weekend in New York City is too short if you want to take advantage of the *great number* of places to visit and things to do there.

10. Greenwich Village has always been considered a good place to live by those who have trouble *adapting to* the norms of society.

F. Express Yourself

1. Do you consider yourself a *conformist* or a *nonconformist*? Explain your answer.

2. *Masterpiece* is a compound word. What does each word mean separately? Think of some *masterpieces* in art, literature, and music.

3. *Launch* can mean more than just to send off physically. Look at the following expressions using *launch* and try to think of the activities which would be involved in the *"launching"*:
   a. to *launch* a new career
   b. to *launch* a new product on the market
   c. to *launch* a political campaign

   Also, in Homer's *The Odyssey,* Helen of Troy was said to have "a face that *launched* a thousand ships." Do you know what this means?

G. Think Back

Answer the following questions according to the text.

1. According to Lisa's letter, what are some of the disadvantages to living in New York City?

2. Who are the Guardian Angels and what do they do?

3. According to Lisa, in what way has the attitude of Americans toward their origins changed?

4. What does Lisa mean when she says that her sister has "the city at her doorstep"?

5. Think of the places in New York City mentioned in the letter. Which would you classify as part of historical New York? Which as part of modern New York? Explain your choices.

H. Talk About It

1. In your own words, express the last part of the inscription of the Statue of Liberty, and explain how it relates to the history of United States immigration.

2. Are you from a major city in your native country? If so, how do the advantages and disadvantages of living there compare to those of living in New York City? If not, does New York City sound like the type of place where you would like to live?

3. The Guardian Angels have been accused of being a vigilante group, in other words, a volunteer group of concerned citizens who are organized to suppress and punish crime, especially when the police seem inadequate. How do you feel about citizens taking the law into their own hands? What are the dangers? Is this really necessary in today's society?

I. Words, Words, Words!

The following vocabulary items have been taken from Lisa's article. Try to guess the meaning of each word from the context and write your definition in the space provided. When you have finished, check the vocabulary list at the end of the book for the correct meaning.

1. controversial _____
   Abortion is a *controversial* subject that has caused many arguments in Congress.

2. conversion _____
   The *conversion* of an increasing number of apartments into privately owned condominiums is opposed by renters in New York and other large American cities.

3. disposal _____

   Garbage *disposal* is a big problem for large cities like New York, which do not know what to do with all their waste.

4. evacuate _____

   After it had rained for four days, the Potomac River was so high that people had to *evacuate* the small town.

5. extended _____

   Detroit is now producing cars that can go for *extended* distances on one tank of gas.

6. extensive _____

   Thanks to Steve's *extensive* explanation of the New York subway system, Lisa found getting around in the city to be easy.

7. lethal _____

   Automobile engines produce carbon monoxide, a *lethal* gas, which poisons the air.

8. outcome _____

   The *outcome* of the five-year traffic study was to build a new bridge across the Hudson River.

9. postponed _____

   The baseball game between the New York Yankees and Boston Red Sox was *postponed* until the following day because of rain.

10. potentially _____

    In certain sections of New York City, walking alone at night is *potentially* dangerous.

11. remote _____

    It takes several hours to fly from New York to the *remote* island of Newfoundland in the North Atlantic.

12. resemble _____

    Lisa couldn't believe how much the salesman at Macy's *resembled* Steve; they could have been brothers.

13. risky _____

    Leaving your car unlocked in a city is *risky*; you may find it gone when you return.

14. sensible _____

    It is more *sensible* to use public transportation than to drive in New York City.

15. spoiled _____

    Litterbugs have *spoiled* many once beautiful beaches on Long Island.

A poster at a subway stop.

J. Headline

FUELS OF THE FUTURE?

by Lisa Evans

1   "This could be the end!" warned the headlines on March 28, 1979, just after the world's worst nuclear power plant accident had occurred at Three-Mile-Island near Harrisburg, Pennsylvania. Children and pregnant women within a five-mile radius of the plant were advised to evacuate the area. In all, over 140,000 people in the vi-

cinity of the plant packed their bags and left their homes and jobs, while millions of others all along the East Coast worried about the possible outcome. Fortunately, despite serious damage to the plant estimated at 2 to 4 billion dollars, most of the radiation was contained. Nevertheless, it will take many years before the total effect on the area's residents and environment can be determined.

2   As the world's supplies of fossil[1] fuels, including oil, coal, and natural gas, continue to shrink, countries are trying to develop alternate energy sources. One of the most controversial solutions to this growing problem lies in nuclear energy.

3   At present the construction of nuclear power plants in the United States has almost reached a standstill. Plans for many nuclear facilities have been postponed or even cancelled as a result of both the declining demand for electricity and strong public opposition. People are becoming increasingly concerned about the dangers that accompany nuclear power.

4   There are two major problems associated with atomic power plants, the first of which concerns nuclear waste. Atomic reactors produce waste products that remain radioactive and potentially lethal for thousands of years. As yet, no safe method has been found for the disposal of these wastes. The second problem relates to the danger of an atomic explosion. Many people doubt that an atomic power plant can be operated safely and shut down quickly in an emergency. An electricity-generating plant powered by fossil fuels can be stopped in minutes; however, an atomic power plant is not as easy to control if something goes wrong. It can remain "hot," or radioactive, for days and even months after an accident. In addition, the critics of nuclear energy are concerned with the human factor at power plants. Despite extensive training programs, plant operators can still make mis-

takes. For these reasons, critics worried about public safety believe the risks associated with nuclear energy are too great to justify its use.

5   A possible solution to atomic energy problems may lie in nuclear fusion. Fission reactors, which are presently in operation, produce energy by splitting atoms; fusion reactors, on the other hand, create energy by combining atoms. The fusion method appears to be safer, since it does not produce radioactive waste. Experts, however, feel that the technology necessary to make fusion practical is still many years in the future.

6   In search of other energy alternatives, the United States has been developing its synfuels industry, which is the production of synthetic fuels to take the place of oil, coal, and natural gas. One of the new technological processes deals with the production of gasohol, a mixture of 90 percent gasoline and 10 percent alcohol. There are two types of alcohol used as fuels: ethanol, produced from corn and other grains, and methanol, produced from coal and city wastes. Either can be mixed with gasoline, but ethanol is preferred. The inferior fuel, methanol, can be improved by extra refining processes, but this increases the cost and reduces the energy input-output ratio. Service stations across the country are already selling gasohol. Despite discouragement from many large oil companies, ethanol may provide a sensible, quick alternative to fossil fuels.

7   Still another alternative to fossil fuels can be found in energy from the sun. Solar energy provides a good source of heat that can be collected and even stored for later use. Already many homes and office buildings have been designed to take advantage of the sun's warmth.

8   The sun can also be used to produce electricity. Solar energy generators are already providing power for remote Indian

villages in Arizona and communities in Alaska. Solar-generated electricity also may be the airplane fuel of the future. Solar-powered aircraft have succeeded in crossing the English Channel and eventually may become practical for extended distances, as more efficient, lighter, and cheaper solar components are developed.

9 People are also turning to a traditional source of power—the wind. Windmills have been used to harness energy from the wind for years. Today, companies are developing power-producing wind machines, such as the two-million-dollar windmill built near Palm Springs, California, where the wind averages 17 miles per hour. This one windmill is expected to provide enough power for almost 1000 homes. Like all sources of energy, though, wind power is not free from criticism. While its proponents argue that it is clean, free, and limitless, there are those who claim that the turbines cause noise pollution, spoil the countryside, and present a danger to flying birds.

10 At one time, renewable energy sources were considered risky. Now many people believe that power generated from the sun, wind and other alternate sources must be developed and relied upon to provide a significant portion of our energy needs. Otherwise, who knows what the outcome will be when the world's supplies of fossil fuels are gone?

Notes

1. fossil: the remains of an ancient plant or animal which have been preserved in the ground.

K. First Impressions

Do the following exercise without referring to the article. Circle the letter next to the statement that best answers the question.

1. Which of the following statements about the accident at Three-Mile-Island is false?
   a. It occurred in Pennsylvania.
   b. Little radiation escaped.
   c. Damage to the plant was minimal.
   d. The effect on the area's population is not clear.

2. According to the article, fewer nuclear plants are being constructed in the United States because of
   a. a declining demand for electricity.
   b. the discovery of new reserves of oil in the Atlantic Ocean.
   c. public opposition.
   d. both a and c.
   e. both b and c.

3. Fusion is
   a. a process that combines atoms.
   b. a process that splits atoms.
   c. presently a practical solution to the energy problem.
   d. both a and c.

4. Which of the following is a false statement?
   a. Gasohol is presently being sold in some service stations.
   b. Ethanol comes from corn.
   c. Methanol cannot be used as a fuel.
   d. Many oil companies are not in favor of gasohol.

5. Proponents of wind power state that it is
   a. noisy.
   b. unattractive.
   c. dangerous for birds.
   d. limitless.

L. Rapid Reading

Do this exercise in class. Scan the article quickly to find the following pieces of information. Write down the number of the paragraph in which each topic is discussed.

a. _____ solar energy: a source of heat

b. _____ nuclear waste

c. _____ wind power

d. _____ fusion

e. _____ solar energy: a source of electricity

f. _____ Three-Mile-Island

g. _____ gasohol

M. Between the Lines

Circle the letter next to the statement that best answers the question. You may refer to the text.

1. What is the main idea of the article?
   a. Possible alternate sources of energy.
   b. The dangers of nuclear power.
   c. Solar power: a solution to the energy crisis.
   d. The world will soon have no more sources of energy.

2. "Fossil fuels" are
   a. a possible solution to the energy crisis.

b. alternate energy sources.

c. fuels, such as coal, which were made from living things.

d. synfuels.

3. In paragraph 4, sentence 1, "which" refers to
   a. atomic power plants.
   b. nuclear waste.
   c. major problems.
   d. atomic reactors.

4. The article implies but does not directly state that
   a. the construction of nuclear power plants has increased steadily in the United States.
   b. fusion produces radioactive waste.
   c. the majority of people in the United States are in favor of nuclear power.
   d. a few nuclear power plants are still being built in the United States

5. Lisa's attitude in the article is best described as
   a. antisolar.
   b. impartial.
   c. pronuclear.
   d. covert.

N. More Expressions

Fill in the blanks with words from the following list. Use the correct voice, tense, and singular or plural form of the noun.

controversial	risky	remote
to evacuate	to resemble	outcome
potentially	to spoil	extensive
	to postpone	

1. Our sailing trip on Chesapeake Bay ＿＿＿＿＿＿＿ because of high winds. We decided to go next week.

2. Despite Steve's ＿＿＿＿＿＿＿ instructions, Lisa couldn't find the restaurant he had recommended in New York City.

3. The Supreme Court in Washington, D.C. has to decide on many ＿＿＿＿＿＿＿ issues.

4. Many city dwellers like to spend their vacations at _____ mountain resorts in the Poconos away from the busy life of the city.

5. The _____ of our discussion was to spend another day in Philadelphia before driving to Baltimore.

6. Many towns along the East Coast _____ last August by the National Guard because of hurricane warnings.

7. The Atlantic Ocean is a(n) _____ rich source of oil.

8. The sidewalk cafés of Greenwich Village _____ those of the Latin Quarter in Paris.

9. Lisa's visit to Atlantic City _____ when she lost $100 at a gambling casino.

10. Playing the stock market on Wall Street can be _____ unless you know what you are doing.

O. Express Yourself

1. Think of some current issues in the news. Which ones are *potentially controversial*? What are some topics which will always be *controversial*?

2. Which sports do you consider *risky*? What are the *risks* involved?

3. *Spoil* can be used in many different contexts. What do you think it means in the following examples:
   a. the food will *spoil*
   b. a *spoiled* child
   c. the *spoils* of war

P. Talk It Up

1. What are "renewable" energy sources?

2. What is the "human factor" associated with nuclear power plants?

3. Where does the word "gasohol" come from? Why do you think many large oil companies discourage the use of gasohol?

4. The article states that refining methanol reduces its energy input-output ratio. What does this mean?

5. Can you think of other alternate sources of energy not mentioned in the article?

6. People waste energy every day. Make a list of at least five energy-saving ideas by yourself or with your classmates.

Q. Word Families

Choose the appropriate form of the word. Be certain to use the correct verb tense, singular or plural form of the noun, and the passive voice where necessary.

1. association, to associate, associated
   a. One _____ Thomas Edison with the light bulb.
   b. An _____ of thirteen colonies formed the original United States.
   c. Independence Hall in Philadelphia is _____ with the Declaration of Independence and the Liberty Bell.

2. despite, in spite
   a. When we were in New York, we went for a walk in Central Park _____ the bad weather.
   b. We had a good time _____ of the rain.

3. reliance, reliability, to rely, reliable, reliant
   a. An alcoholic _____ upon alcohol to get through the day.
   b. A _____ upon alcohol is not good for a person's physical or mental health.
   c. New York City is _____ upon water from the Catskill Mountains.
   d. The Chesapeake Bay is a _____ source of soft-shelled crabs.
   e. Lisa questioned the _____ of her road map; it was five years old.

4. opponent, opposition, to oppose, opposing, opposed
   a. There is a lot of _____ to nuclear power in the United States.
   b. The _____ of nuclear power feel that it is extremely dangerous.
   c. They _____ the construction of new nuclear plants.
   d. Most power companies, however, hold an _____ view.
   e. They are not _____ to nuclear power and feel that it is a necessary source of energy for the United States.

5. spectacle, spectator, spectacular, spectacularly
   a. The nation's capital celebrated the country's two-hundredth birthday on July 4, 1976, with a _____ fireworks display.
   b. People came from all over the country to celebrate and view the _____.
   c. The cherry trees that blossom every spring along the Potomac River in Washington are _____ beautiful.
   d. _____ are welcome to observe the proceedings in the United States Senate and House of Representatives.

6. controversy, controversial
   a. There is a great deal of _____ surrounding the use of solar power.
   b. Its critics feel that the _____ source of energy is not practical at present.

7. disposal, to dispose, disposable
   a. The _____ of hot water is a problem for nuclear plants.
   b. The hot water can kill fish and plant life if nuclear facilities _____ of it directly into rivers and streams.
   c. Many states have banned the use of _____ bottles for beer and soft drinks.

8. pollution, pollutant, polluter, to pollute, polluted
   a. Air _____ is a problem along the densely populated East Coast.
   b. The automobile is the major air _____.
   c. Nitrogen oxides and carbon monoxide are two _____ in the air.
   d. Factory smoke and automobile exhaust combine with water droplets in the air to form "acid rain," which _____ lakes, rivers, and streams.
   e. _____ air is particularly bad for people with respiratory problems.

9. attraction, to attract, attractive, attractively
   a. Historical Philadelphia, Pennsylvania _____ hundreds of thousands of tourists every year.
   b. One of the city's leading _____ is Independence Hall where the Declaration of Independence was signed in 1776.
   c. It is pleasant to walk among the _____ brick homes in Philadelphia's old residential districts.
   d. The _____ decorated restaurant near the city's historical area specialized in serving a delicious Sunday brunch.

10. (non)conformist, conformity, to conform
    a. The early American patriots did not want _____ to the laws and wishes of England.

b. _____ to the laws of the church was required in many colonial villages.

c. The young business executive was a _____; he refused to wear a suit and tie to work like everyone else did.

R. Look It Up

1. Who are the Quakers and which state was named after one of their leaders?

2. Where did the Statue of Liberty come from?

3. Who is Rip Van Winkle and what is his story?

4. Why do you think Philadelphia, Pennsylvania is called the "Cradle of the Nation"?

5. What is "Wall Street" and how did it get its name?

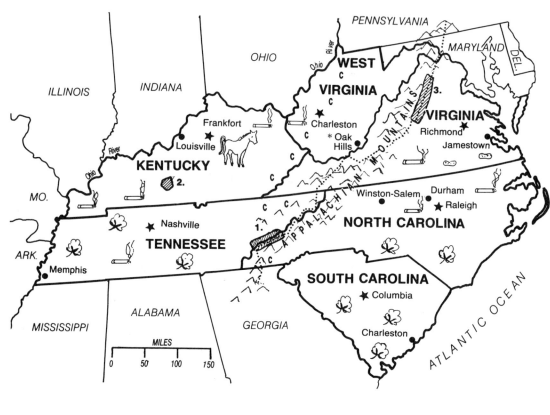

ILLINOIS

INDIANA

OHIO

PENNSYLVANIA

MARYLAND

DEL.

WEST VIRGINIA

c

c

Charleston
* Oak Hills

c

VIRGINIA

Richmond ★
Jamestown

Frankfort ★
Louisville

KENTUCKY

2.

MO.

c

c

c

c

Winston-Salem

Durham
★ Raleigh

NORTH CAROLINA

3.

ARK.

Nashville ★

TENNESSEE

1.

Memphis

c

c

SOUTH CAROLINA
★ Columbia

Charleston

MISSISSIPPI

ALABAMA

GEORGIA

ATLANTIC OCEAN

MILES

0   50   100   150

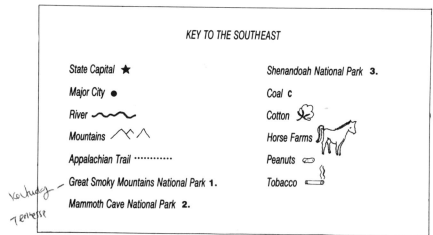

KEY TO THE SOUTHEAST

State Capital ★

Major City ●

River ～～～

Mountains ∧∧ ∧

Appalachian Trail ·········

Great Smoky Mountains National Park **1.**

Mammoth Cave National Park **2.**

Shenandoah National Park **3.**

Coal **c**

Cotton

Horse Farms

Peanuts

Tobacco

Kentucky —

Tennesse

chapter 3

The Southeast

West Virginia
Virginia
1 Centucky
Tenesse
north carolina
South carolina

A. Take a Look

I. Answer the following questions by looking at the map:

1. What is the capital of Kentucky? *Louisville*

2. In which state is Memphis?

3. Which states form Virginia's southern border?

4. What is West Virginia's primary industry?

5. How many states touch the Atlantic Ocean?

6. Where are most of the horse farms located?

II. Make up questions that could be answered by the following information:

1. Columbia

2. West of North Carolina and south of Kentucky

3. On the border of Tennessee and North Carolina

4. In North and South Carolina and Tennessee

5. The Ohio River

*Oak Hills is a fictitious but typical town of the Southeast.

B. A Letter from Lisa

Oak Hills, West Virginia
June 17

Dear Steve,

On my way south I decided to take some time off and travel through the heart of Appalachia. For the past few days, I've been staying in Oak Hills, West Virginia, a small town of about 350 residents. There are no hotels here, but I was able to rent a small room in a Mrs. Davies' home for next to nothing.

I have no real explanation for why I chose Oak Hills. I guess I just wanted to see Appalachia, that mountainous region of the Southeast which so many people associate with the stereotype of hillbillies,[1] moonshine,[2] and poverty.

Oak Hills is one of many mining communities in this region. In some ways, it's a very sobering place to visit. Yesterday I met a former coal miner who is suffering from black lung, a disease which totally incapacitates its victims. The disease is caused by a buildup of coal dust in the lungs and is a frequent, cruel reward for those who've spent many years working in the mines. But the miners, and the people of Oak Hills in general, seem to take a fatalistic approach to life. Coal mining is their life's work—and, for many, their life's end. According to statistics, coal mining is the most dangerous profession in the U.S. Yet sons replace fathers in the mines while everyone continues to hope for safer and better working conditions. Supposedly, conditions are getting better, but there still seems to be room for improvement.

These past few days I've been wondering why the people of Oak Hills don't get tired of this rugged, cruel life. They don't seem to miss the conveniences and luxuries we associate with modern living. Instead, they're fiercely proud and strongly attached to their land—to the incredible beauty of moonlit ridges and gentle valleys.

You know, I've become quite fond of Mrs. Davies. She'll be 82 years old next month and is still quilting[3]—not to mention cooking, cleaning, and gardening! She makes the most beautiful patchwork quilts[4] I've ever seen. Her only worry in life is that "not enough young folk are learnin'[5] to quilt," and she's afraid it'll become a lost art.

Somehow I don't think so. The young people here are very conscious of the value of their customs and heritage. They're proud to carry on in the same traditions as their parents.

And they have a lot to be proud of, too. Many of Oak Hills' citizens are not only miners or skilled crafts people but fine musicians as well. Last Saturday night the whole town got together for an evening of "bluegrass and clogging." The fiddle and banjo, both so characteristic of this region, combined with other instruments to produce the most "toe tappin', foot stompin'" music I've ever heard. The people jumped to their feet and started clogging, a spirited dance that goes with bluegrass music. I found out that you don't become an accomplished "clogger" overnight, but I <u>did</u> manage to learn a few steps. It's impossible to sit still when that music's being played!

Tomorrow I say good-bye to Oak Hills, and it's on to Durham, the motel room and my typewriter. I'll really miss Mrs. Davies and all the people I've met here. As I travel through the different states, I realize that it's not just the scenery that changes. Until now, I never really appreciated the variety of traditions and lifestyles in our United States. Just like Mrs. Davies' patchwork quilts of colorful pieces of cloth, the U.S. is made of its own patchwork of people and places. Each of the pieces has its own unique character, but somehow, in the end, they all fit together.

Next letter from Florida,

Notes

1. hillbilly: a person from a backwoods area, particularly Appalachia, who has little contact with urban lifestyles.
2. moonshine: a whiskey with a very high alcohol content which is made at home and illegal if sold.
3. quilting: a special process of sewing together layers of cloth to make various patterns.
4. patchwork quilts: blankets made of different pieces of cloth sewn together into a colorful pattern.
5. In many regional dialects the final "g" of the present participle of the verb is dropped in informal speech.

C. True or False?

Write T before those statements that are true and F before those that are false.

_____ 1. Lisa's room in Mrs. Davies' home was free.
_____ 2. Black lung is a relatively common disease among miners.
_____ 3. Working conditions in the mines are getting better.
_____ 4. Lisa thinks that the people of Oak Hills are tired of their lifestyle and would like to leave Appalachia.
_____ 5. Mrs. Davies spends the entire day quilting.
_____ 6. Lisa thinks that the young people of Oak Hills are proud of their heritage and traditions.
_____ 7. Lisa quickly became an expert clogger.

_____ 8. Mrs. Davies' only worry is that someday no one will know how to quilt anymore.

_____ 9. Lisa went to Oak Hills to do research for her article on tobacco.

_____ 10. The stereotype of Appalachia includes beautiful beaches and wealth.

D. Close-up

Fill in the blanks with a, an, or the. If no article is necessary, put an X in the blank.

Lisa rented _____ room from _____ Mrs. Davies because _____ small
              (1)   (2)   (3)

town she was visiting had no hotels. Mrs. Davies was _____ amazing
              (4)

82-year-old woman with many talents. _____ beautiful patchwork quilts
              (5)

covered every bed in _____ house. Outside there was _____ small
              (6)   (7)

garden filled with _____ flowers and _____ vegetables. Mrs. Davies
              (8)   (9)

was also _____ excellent cook. Lisa thought _____ woman she was
       (10)   (11)

staying with was one of _____ nicest people she'd ever met!
             (12)

E. Expressions

Rewrite the following sentences, replacing the italicized words with the correct form of the appropriate word or expression.

to take time off	room for improvement	accomplished
convenience	sobering	fatalistic
supposedly	to incapacitate	reward
	stereotype	

1. Mrs. Davies' nephew *was disabled* by a severe automobile accident last year in the Great Smoky Mountains of Tennessee.

2. Not all of Kentucky's corn is eaten as a vegetable. *It is believed* more than half of it is used to make bourbon whiskey, but no one knows for sure.

3. The *picture that comes to mind* of an Appalachian hillbilly is a person who is ill-mannered and uncultured; however, Lisa found the residents of Oak Hills to be polite and to have a rich local culture.

4. Some of the homes in the hills of West Virginia have no *appliances* to make life easier for their inhabitants.

5. After a few days of clogging to bluegrass music, the sight of her typewriter had a *restraining* effect on Lisa's carefree mood.

6. After their successful hunting trip, the old man tossed the dog a bone as a *gesture of appreciation* for his hard work.

7. Many of the miners Lisa interviewed believed they were powerless to change the course of their lives. They had an *"It's already been decided"* attitude.

8. Life in the hills of Appalachia can be difficult for women as most can't *stop working for a while* when they become mothers, but must continue with their jobs instead.

9. Although Lisa had become fairly good at clogging she still felt there was *the possibility of becoming better at it.*

10. Stephen Foster, a *skilled* musician from Kentucky, wrote more than 50 melodies, including the popular "My Old Kentucky Home."

F. Express Yourself

1. What's the *stereotype* of an American in your native country? Ask your classmates about the *stereotype* people have of someone from *your* native country. Do you fit it?

2. Would you like to *take some time off* from work or school? If so, what would you do?

3. Are you a *fatalist* or do you believe that you can control your own destiny?

G. Think Back

Answer the following questions according to the text.

1. Why does Lisa consider Oak Hills a sobering place to visit?

2. What does Mrs. Davies spend her day doing?

3. Name two musical instruments that are characteristic of bluegrass music.

4. How does Lisa describe Appalachia?

5. To what does Lisa compare the United States and why?

H. Talk About It

1. Bluegrass music is representative of the southeastern region of the United States. What type of music is representative of your native country?

2. Does Appalachia sound like the type of place where you'd like to live? Why or why not?

I. Words, Words, Words!

The following vocabulary items have been taken from Lisa's article. Try to guess the meaning of each word from the context and write your definition in the space provided. When you have finished, check the vocabulary list at the end of the book for the correct meaning.

1. advocate_____
   The senator from North Carolina who opposed abortion was an *advocate* of the "right to life" movement.

2. challenge_____
   The white water of the New River in West Virginia is a *challenge* for even highly skilled canoeists and rafters.

3. consumption_____
   Oil *consumption* has decreased in the United States in contrast to that of gas and coal.

4. cut down on (something)_____
   In order to *cut down on* heating expenses, many people throughout Appalachia have returned to using wood stoves.

5. drowsiness_____
   It is dangerous to drive a car when taking any medication that causes *drowsiness*; you could fall asleep at the wheel.

6. link_____
   The *link* between coal dust and black lung disease was obvious when large numbers of miners became sick with the disease.

7. lucrative_____
   Raising horses can be a *lucrative* business. Horse sales in Kentucky exceed $200 million annually.

8. nontoxic_____

People searching for mushrooms in the hills of Appalachia must be careful; some of the mushrooms are *nontoxic,* but others are poisonous.

9. quit_____

The racehorse had to *quit* racing for several months after it had injured its ankle.

10. symptom_____

The owner of the general store in Oak Hills had all the *symptoms* of a bad allergy: sneezing, headache, and watery eyes.

11. unaware_____

Never having visited Mammoth Cave, Lisa was *unaware* that the cave had over 200 miles of caverns.

J. Headline

AFTER A CENTURY OF SMOKING, IS IT TIME TO QUIT?

by Lisa Evans

1   On a warm summer day the sweet smell of raw tobacco is heavy in the air. Outside the city, enormous warehouses[1] stretch for miles, ready to supply the ever-productive factories with endless quantities of tobacco. In the heart of the city, neat, red-brick factories house dozens of machines, each of which can produce more than 4,200 cigarettes a minute. Everywhere there are car bumper stickers that read "Enjoy tobacco products." This is Durham, North Carolina, the unofficial capital of the American cigarette industry and just one of the many locations in the South where tobacco is king.

2   North American Indians had been growing tobacco in the sandy, red soil of the Southeast for centuries before the English first arrived in the early 1600s. The English colonists, who knew of the large European market for tobacco and recognized the potential profit, quickly began cultivating the lucrative crop themselves. Over the decades, tobacco consumption remained fairly constant; however, in the late 1800s two separate changes in the industry caused a sharp rise in the sale of cigarettes.

3   In 1875, a company in Virginia offered the huge sum of $75,000 to anyone who could invent a machine for mass producing cigarettes. At that time, cigarettes were still being rolled by hand in the factories; this process, of course, made them very expensive. Since most smokers could not afford the luxury of factory-made cigarettes, they brought paper and tobacco and rolled their own. James Bonsack, an enterprising teenager from Virginia, accepted the company's challenge. Against his father's wishes, he dropped out of college and spent the next five years working on his invention. In 1880, "the Bonsack," as he called his machine, was finished. With this machine, tobacco flowed evenly onto a long,

narrow strip of paper which was then rolled tightly into a single tube. As the tobacco-filled tube left the machine, it was cut into cigarettes of equal length. Bonsack's invention revolutionized the cigarette industry. One machine could do the work of 48 factory workers, thus making inexpensive cigarettes a possibility.

4   The method of processing cigarette tobacco also changed significantly in the 1870s. Until that time, tobacco leaves, after being harvested, were simply hung up to dry in barns, a process called curing. Tobacco growers discovered that heating the leaves during the curing process produced a milder, more pleasant-tasting tobacco. The new process gradually caught on among tobacco growers, and by 1880 it had become standard procedure. As a direct result of this change in curing which altered the composition of the tobacco, cigarette smoke became milder, easier to inhale, and more addictive. A century of tobacco addiction had begun.

5   The early tobacco growers and cigarette manufacturers were unaware of the hidden dangers of their product. It was not until much later that the health hazards associated with smoking were discovered. The first studies that suggested a link between smoking and illness were made public in 1953 and 1954. Since then, research has clearly established this relationship. Studies have shown that nicotine and carbon monoxide, two poisons contained in cigarette smoke, are responsible for heart disease—the primary cause of death among smokers. In addition, research has indicated that lung cancer, the second leading cause of death among smokers, results from the buildup of tars, small organic particles in cigarette smoke. It has also been found that smoking is especially dangerous during pregnancy. The babies of women who smoke have a higher mortality rate and are more likely to be premature or smaller at birth than the babies of nonsmoking mothers.

6   In 1911, Americans smoked almost 10 billion cigarettes. Sixty years later this number approached 700 billion. Despite this amazing increase, the demand for cigarettes in the United States is now gradually dropping. Since 1973, per capita cigarette consumption has decreased approximately 1 percent annually. According to some estimates, 90 percent of all cigarette smokers would like to cut down or quit smoking entirely, but that, of course, is not easy to do and many do not succeed.

7   Smokers who try to "kick the habit" may experience both physical and psychological withdrawal[2] symptoms for several weeks. They may suffer, for example, from headaches, nausea, irritability, and an inability to concentrate. Some symptoms, such as drowsiness and craving (a strong desire for a cigarette), get even worse after the first ten days. Most people continue to crave cigarettes for at least a month, and approximately one-fifth continue to desire them for as many as five to nine *years* after they have quit.

8   As the American people have become increasingly conscious of good health habits, their attitudes toward smoking have changed. Nonsmokers are demanding the right to breathe smokeless, nontoxic air, especially since recent studies have indicated that secondhand smoke, that is, the cigarette smoke in the air, is potentially dangerous. Gradually, the demands of anti-smoking advocates are getting results. Some cities, such as Eugene, Oregon, have already passed strict laws that require restaurants to provide nonsmoking sections. It seems that smoking is no longer considered socially acceptable behavior by many in American society.

(Courtesy R.J. Reynolds Tobacco Company)

Will this machine ever stop?

[handwritten margin notes:]
anecdote = little story
to chain smoke.
"Cold turkey" ↑ completely quit smoking

to catch on : to become popular / to understand (to learn something.
curing : process that changes quality.
per capita : per each person

Notes

1. warehouse: a building for storing materials and merchandise.
2. withdrawal: the process of giving up an addictive substance.

K. First Impressions

Do the following exercise without referring to the article. Circle the letter next to the statement that best answers the question.

1. In the late 1800s, the cigarette industry experienced a sharp rise in sales due to
   a. the invention of "the Bonsack."
   b. the addition of nicotine to tobacco.

c. a change in the process of curing tobacco.

d. both a and b.

e. both a and c.

2. Tobacco was first grown in the United States by
   a. English colonists.
   b. North American Indians.
   c. the Bonsacks.
   d. the Virginians.

3. Which of the following components of cigarette smoke is supposedly responsible for lung cancer?
   a. tar
   b. nicotine
   c. carbon dioxide
   d. carbon monoxide

4. According to the article, per capita cigarette consumption in the United States
   a. cannot be measured.
   b. is increasing.
   c. is decreasing.
   d. is remaining constant.

5. Which of the following statements is false?
   a. Americans are smoking less because they are more conscious of good health.
   b. Smoking is no longer considered totally acceptable behavior by many in the United States.
   c. Early tobacco growers were aware of the dangers of their product.
   d. Some people who have quit smoking crave a cigarette for as many as nine years.

L. Rapid Reading

Do this exercise in class. Scan the article quickly to find the following pieces of information. Write down the number of the paragraph in which each topic is discussed.

a. _____ the poisons contained in cigarette smoke

b. _____ the mass production of cigarettes

c. _____ possible withdrawal symptoms

d. _____ the curing process

e. _____ the attitude of nonsmokers

M. Between the Lines

Circle the letter next to the statement that best answers the question. You may refer to the text.

1. What is the main idea of the article?
   a. The health hazards of smoking.
   b. The history of cigarette smoking in the United States.
   c. "The Bonsack"—the first machine for mass producing cigarettes.
   d. The nonsmoking trend in the United States.

2. In paragraph 3, the article states that Bonsack's machine revolutionized the cigarette industry. In this context, "revolutionized" means
   a. caused factory workers to organize labor unions.
   b. made it possible for the cigarette industry to take over the world.
   c. changed the industry significantly.

3. In paragraph 5, sentence 1, "their" refers to
   a. cigarette manufacturers.
   b. tobacco growers.
   c. both a and b.

4. In the context of paragraph 7, the phrase "to kick the habit" means
   a. to stop smoking.
   b. to complain about the effects of cigarettes.
   c. to smoke more cigarettes.
   d. to exercise too much.

5. In paragraph 4, the article states that the new curing process gradually caught on among tobacco growers. In this context, "caught on" means
   a. understood.
   b. became popular.
   c. was considered satisfactory.

6. The main idea of paragraph 8 is
   a. new laws have been passed to restrict cigarette smoking.
   b. secondhand smoke is dangerous.
   c. many Americans are adopting a negative attitude toward cigarette smoking.

N. More Expressions

Fill in the blanks with words from the following list. Use the correct voice, tense, and singular or plural form of the noun.

challenge	to cut down on	consumption
symptom	unaware (of)	to quit
drowsiness	lucrative	advocate
	link	

1. Selling moonshine whiskey is an illegal but often _____ business.

2. The covert production and _____ of moonshine whiskey increased during the years of Prohibition (1919–1933), when all alcoholic beverages were illegal.

3. Although Lisa enjoyed Southern cooking very much, she decided _____ her daily number of calories so she would not gain weight.

4. After the woman described her numerous _____, the doctor gave her a prescription for drugs.

5. "It's easy _____ smoking. I've done it hundreds of times!"

6. _____ is the cause of many automobile accidents on winding mountain roads.

7. Ralph Nader, a well-known consumer _____, has worked hard to improve the quality of various products on the market.

8. Travelers from the North who are _____ the fact that tobacco is cured by smoke often call farmers to tell them their barns are on fire.

9. Daily ferries provide a(n) _____ between the picturesque North Carolina island of Ocracoke and the mainland.
[Okrokoki]

10. Trying to study for your English exam while your roommate is having a wild party is really a(n) _____.

O. Express Yourself

(handwritten annotations at top: innoculation (shot) / immunization / tuberculoses / polio)

1. Lisa caught a bad cold while she was traveling down the East Coast. What do you think her *symptoms* were? What *symptoms* would you have for the flu? For the measles? For the mumps? *(handwritten: Swollen jaws / fever)*

2. Pretend you're going on a diet. What are some foods you will have to *cut down on*? What will you replace them with?

3. Look at question number 10 above. Use your imagination to come up with some other interesting *challenges*!

P. Talk It Up

1. What are some of the withdrawal symptoms that people who quit smoking experience?

2. What seems to be the current attitude toward smoking in the United States? In your native country?

3. Why do you think people continue to smoke when research has clearly linked smoking to bad health?

4. The United States government has banned cigarette commercials from radio and television. Is this in contradiction to the right to free speech guaranteed by the United States Constitution? What do you think?

5. A new smoking trend is surfacing in the United States. While tobacco smoking has lost in popularity, the use of marijuana has steadily gained. The illegal marijuana trade with multi-billion-dollar sales is presently rivaling the automobile and tobacco industries. Should marijuana eventually be legalized and allowed to join alcohol and tobacco as an accepted national habit?

Q. Word Families

Choose the appropriate form of the word. Be certain to use the correct verb tense, singular or plural form of the noun, and the passive voice where necessary.

1. irritation, to irritate, irritating, irritable
   a. Cigarette smoke _____ the throat and lungs.
   b. Contact lens wearers often find the smoke especially _____ to their eyes, too.
   c. Having to dine in a restaurant next to a table of smokers is a source of _____ for many nonsmokers.
   d. Lisa is sometimes _____ in the morning if she has not had enough sleep and her cup of coffee.

2. consumption, consumer, to consume
    a. Mrs. Davies was busy quilting when she finally remembered her cake in the oven—but too late! It was no longer fit for human _____.

    b. In order to stay cool on hot days in the South, people _____ large quantities of cold drinks.

    c. Increased production costs for furniture made in North Carolina are passed on to _____ in the form of higher prices.

3. withdrawal, to withdraw, withdrawn
    a. Before leaving Boston, Lisa _____ money from her bank account and bought traveler's checks.

    b. Her account was considerably smaller after this _____.

    c. The shy mountain woman, who was not accustomed to strangers, was very _____ when the out-of-state tourists stopped to ask for directions.

4. (in)convenience, (in)convenient, (in)conveniently
    a. Modern smokers prefer the _____ of prerolled cigarettes.

    b. They find it _____ to carry tobacco and papers.

    c. Consequently, most tobacco is sold in _____ packaged cigarettes.

5. resident, residence, to reside, residential
    a. The people that _____ in Appalachia still practice century-old crafts and skills.

    b. The _____ of Charleston, South Carolina are very proud of their beautiful city.

    c. The _____ area along the waterfront has many fine mansions from the eighteenth century.

    d. Some of the stately, old _____ are open to the public.

6. awareness, to beware, aware, unaware
    a. The sign on the fence around the dilapidated house read, "_____ of the dog! "

    b. Thanks to the American Cancer Association, most smokers today are at least _____ of the dangers of smoking.

    c. Lisa's _____ of cultural differences between areas in the United States had increased while she was traveling.

    d. Until Lisa visited Oak Hills, she was _____ of the existence of the disease called black lung.

7. former, formerly, formal, formally
    a. _____ invitations to the reception at the Governor's mansion in Raleigh were sent to important North Carolinian political figures.

    b. Guests were asked to dress _____ for the reception.

    c. The capital of North Carolina was _____ located in New Bern.

d. One of Lisa's _____ professors was teaching at Duke University in Durham.

8. significance, to signify, significant, significantly
   a. There were _____ differences between Lisa's lifestyle and Mrs. Davies', but the two got along very well.
   b. Orville and Wilbur Wright _____ altered the course of history on December 17, 1903, at Kitty Hawk, North Carolina, when their "flying machine" actually left the ground and flew.
   c. The world recognized the _____ of what was man's first powered flight.
   d. The Wright brothers' success _____ the beginning of a new era in transportation.

9. recognition, to recognize, recognizable, recognized
   a. Nashville, Tennessee is the _____ capital of country and western music.
   b. When she was listening to live music from the Grand Ole Opry on the radio, Lisa _____ the voice of singer Loretta Lynn.
   c. A memorial was built at Kitty Hawk in _____ of the Wright brothers' achievement.
   d. From his strong accent the man was easily _____ as a native of South Carolina.

10. invention, inventor, to invent, inventive
    a. Eli Whitney _____ the cotton gin in the late eighteenth century.
    b. His _____ mechanized the process of cleaning rough cotton after it had been picked.
    c. The _____ was born in Massachusetts.
    d. His _____ skills led to inexpensive cotton fabrics and made him internationally famous.

R. Look It Up

1. Look in your dictionary and find the origin of the word "hillbilly." How do you think "moonshine" got its name? What is a "Tennessee Walker"?

2. Look up information on the Appalachian Trail. If you followed it from start to finish, which states would you pass through?

3. Find Jamestown, Virginia on the map. Why is it important in American history?

4. What is the Kentucky Derby? Kentucky bourbon?

5. Who was Daniel Boone? Davy Crockett?

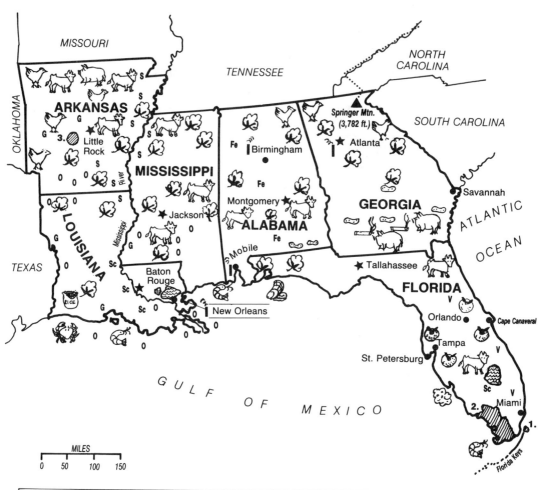

MISSOURI

TENNESSEE

NORTH CAROLINA

SOUTH CAROLINA

OKLAHOMA

ARKANSAS

Little Rock **3.**

River

MISSISSIPPI

Springer Mtn. (3,782 ft.)

Atlanta

Fe

Birmingham

Jackson

Montgomery

ALABAMA

Fe

GEORGIA

Savannah

ATLANTIC OCEAN

TEXAS

LOUISIANA

Mississippi

Baton Rouge

Sc

Mobile

New Orleans

Tallahassee

FLORIDA

Orlando

Cape Canaveral

Tampa

St. Petersburg

GULF   OF   MEXICO

Miami

2.

1.

Florida Keys

MILES

0   50   100   150

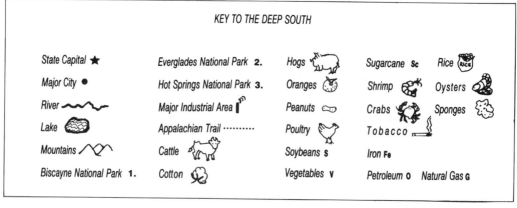

KEY TO THE DEEP SOUTH

State Capital ★

Major City ●

River

Lake

Mountains

Biscayne National Park **1.**

Everglades National Park **2.**

Hot Springs National Park **3.**

Major Industrial Area

Appalachian Trail ··········

Cattle

Cotton

Hogs

Oranges

Peanuts

Poultry

Soybeans **S**

Vegetables **V**

Sugarcane **Sc**

Shrimp

Crabs

Tobacco

Iron **Fe**

Rice

Oysters

Sponges

Petroleum **O**   Natural Gas **G**

chapter 4

The Deep South

A. Take a Look

I. Answer the following questions by looking at the map:

1. Which city has three sets of double letters in its name?
   Tallahassee
2. Which product is most important in the Deep South?
   Cotton
3. Which city is near the mouth of the Mississippi River?
   new orleans
4. Where can you find iron deposits?
5. Which two states have large deposits of petroleum and gas?
6. Which state has the same name as its western border?

II. Make up questions that could be answered by the following information:

1. Biscayne and Everglades
2. Little Rock
3. In southern Alabama and Georgia
4. Oklahoma, Missouri, Texas, Tennessee, Mississippi, and Louisiana
5. The Keys

B. A Letter from Lisa

Clearwater Beach, Florida
June 25

Dear Steve,

Florida in the summertime is too hot and humid for me. Right now the temperature is hovering at 90° and it's only 11:00 A.M.! Thank goodness all the buildings here are air conditioned. I just wish my car were; it's like an oven! Tourists love Florida all year round, but I think I'll save any future trips to the "Sunshine State" for my Christmas vacations.

Since Friday, I've been staying at a motel in Clearwater Beach, near Tampa on the Gulf of Mexico. It's a typical Florida motel, painted pink with white trim and equipped with a swimming pool, even though the beach is just across the street. You know, there's something very predictable about the average motel room in the United States. It always seems to have a color T.V., air conditioning, and two double beds separated by a night table with a Bible and picture postcards featuring the motel in the top drawer. I don't mean to sound too critical. What it lacks in charm and character, it makes up for in dependable comfort.

The beach here is a beautiful, four-mile stretch of powdery, white sand, bordered by graceful palm trees. The water is amazingly warm and swimming is a pleasure. What a change for someone used to a quick dip in the icy Atlantic off the coast of Maine! You have to be careful, though, of the sun, which is so strong that you can end up looking like a boiled lobster after an hour on the beach!

Of course, no trip to Florida would be complete without a visit to Walt Disney World in Orlando, where I spent a couple of days before coming here. I'm not sure that words can adequately describe that experience. Walt Disney had an incredible ability to combine fantasy with reality, so it's hard to tell where one leaves off and the other begins at Disney World. For example, I treated myself to a night at the Polynesian Resort Hotel, which is built on the edge of the man-made Seven Seas Lagoon.[1] Everything from the thatched[2] roofs to the delicious Polynesian food was authentic, or rather, an authentic copy.

I looked up a few statistics for you, Steve. Walt Disney World covers 43 square miles, or an area about twice the size of Manhattan! It has five lakes, 256 boats (which, I've been told, give it the world's tenth largest navy), three golf courses, two railroads, a monorail, 717 campsites, and a 7500-acre wildlife preserve[3]—in short, an entire recreational area offering every imaginable facility a vacationer could want.

In the Magic Kingdom,[4] which accounts for only a small section of Disney World, you can visit any or all of six "lands": Main Street, U.S.A., where visitors can see America at the turn of the century; Fantasyland, which is populated by "live" Disney characters; Tomorrowland, which offers exciting trips into the future; Adventureland, where people can take a jungle cruise along the rivers of the world; Frontierland, where the Wild West of the nineteenth century comes alive; and finally Liberty Square, a portrayal of colonial America. What I enjoyed most though was my visit to the Hall of Presidents in Liberty Square, where all the American presidents from George Washington on are reunited in time. Who would believe that the Abraham Lincoln giving a speech is really an impostor, a computer controlled robot?[5]

I was also given a tour of the eight-acre basement, which is the "nerve center"[6] of the Magic Kingdom. This isn't a tourist attraction, but it should be. Everything necessary for running the entire amusement park is located here underground; the water lines, the power lines, the employee facilities (including Pluto and Goofy's dressing rooms), and a computer system so elaborate that it controls everything from trash disposal to Lincoln's speech! It's hard to believe this all began with Mickey Mouse!

There are some people, however, who resent the impact Disney World has had on central Florida, and, specifically, on Orlando. Back in 1964, when Walt Disney was secretly purchasing pieces of land for his dream project, Orlando was a relatively quiet community. Today, traffic has become a major problem along with water pollution, sky-high real estate prices, a higher cost of living, and a growing crime rate. Disney World critics claim that Cinderella's castle with its golden towers rules over a kingdom of neon and plastic. While I feel these complaints are valid, I still have to admire Disney's creative genius. Who knows? With the opening of the new Disneyland in Tokyo, Mickey Mouse just may be the next United States ambassador to Japan. How's that for a "Disney World"!

Anyway, tomorrow I'm driving to Cape Canaveral to tour the space center. Did I ever tell you that my secret ambition at age nine was to become an astronaut? I only opted for journalism after I suddenly discovered I didn't really like flying.

By the way, I've sent you your own personalized Mouseketeer hat, complete with Mickey Mouse ears. It was hard to decide between the hat and a pink, plastic flamingo[7] for your front lawn. I hope I made the right choice. Do you wear a "large"?

Y'all[8] take care now,

Notes

1. lagoon: a shallow, artificial pond.
2. thatched: made with a plant material, usually straw.
3. wildlife preserve: an area where wild animals and plants are protected.
4. the Magic Kingdom: the amusement park area of Disney World.

5. robot: a machine that looks like a human being and can perform various tasks.
6. nerve center: a source of control or energy.
7. flamingo: an aquatic bird, found in Florida, with pink feathers and a long neck and legs. Plastic replicas of the bird are sometimes used as garden decorations.
8. y'all: a colloquial Southern contraction for "you all," used even in the singular.

C. True or False?

Write T before those statements that are true and F before those that are false.

_____ 1. Lisa's car doesn't have air conditioning.
_____ 2. Although the Florida sun is hot, the water off the coast is still cold.
_____ 3. Lisa's major criticism of motels in the United States is that they lack comfort.
_____ 4. Winter or summer, Florida is a very popular vacation spot.
_____ 5. Disney World covers an area about twice the size of New York state.
_____ 6. When he was buying land, Walt Disney did not make public his intentions to build a Disney World in Florida.
_____ 7. In Liberty Square, you can see an actor dressed as Abraham Lincoln deliver a speech to a group of American presidents.
_____ 8. Lisa can't understand why people complain about Disney World.
_____ 9. Lisa sent Steve a mouseketeer hat and a pink, plastic flamingo as souvenirs of her trip.
_____ 10. The controls for running Disney World are not in view of the ordinary visitor.

D. Close-up

Fill in the blanks with the appropriate preposition.

Back _____ 1513, Ponce de León, an explorer _____ Spain, came
     (1)   (2)

_____ Florida looking _____ the fountain _____ youth, but _____
(3)   (4)   (5)   (6)

no success; and it seems people have been searching _____ it ever since.
                                                         (7)

Every year, _____ the winter, thousands _____ travelers _____ the
(8)   (9)   (10)

northern states head south _____ Florida. Older people especially are
(11)

attracted _____ the "Sunshine State"; _____ fact, more retired
(12)   (13)

Americans move _____ Florida than _____ any other state in the
(14)   (15)

country. _____ course, the fountain _____ youth still hasn't been
(16)   (17)

found, but no one really seems to care. Just looking _____ it _____
(18)   (19)

sunny Florida is enough.

E. Expressions

Rewrite the following sentences, replacing the italicized words with the correct form of the appropriate word or expression.

to opt	in short	to hover
impact	stretch	predictable
adequately	trim	impostor
	valid	

1. On January 11, 1861, Alabama *made the choice* to join the other Southern states in fighting against the North.

2. The *expanse* of subtropical wilderness covering a large part of southern Florida is known as Everglades National Park.

3. For a short period of time, the hurricane stopped in its northward path and *remained suspended* over Miami, causing severe damage.

4. When Coca-Cola was first served in a drugstore in Atlanta, Georgia over a century ago, no one had any idea of the huge *effect* the drink would have on the beverage industry of the United States.

5. From Disney World, Lisa sent postcards to Alexandra, Amelia, Elliot, Bob, and Steve—*to be brief,* to all her friends at the *Daily.*

6. While Lisa was looking for her car, she saw one almost identical to hers in the parking lot. The only difference was in the *decoration* of the two cars.

7. For many historians, the defeat of the South in the Civil War was *foreseeable* when Vicksburg, Mississippi surrendered to General Grant.

8. The man staying in the hotel at Disney World was supposed to be an important foreign diplomat. Actually, he was a *fake,* born and raised in Jackson, Mississippi.

9. Before heading to the beach for a day in the sun, Lisa made sure she was *sufficiently* prepared; she had her sunglasses, her suntan lotion, and a large beach towel.

10. When Walt Disney was searching for a site with good weather all year round to locate Disney World, Florida was a *legitimate* choice.

F. Express Yourself

1. *Trim* has many different meanings. Use your dictionary to find out what it means in the following contexts:
   a. a *trim* woman
   b. to *trim* a Christmas tree
   c. the *trim* on a dress
   d. to get your hair *trimmed*

2. Was studying English only one of many *options* for you? If so, what were some of your other *options*? Why did you *opt* to learn English rather than another language?

3. A "medium" is a person who supposedly can *predict* future events. Do you think this is possible? By yourself or with some classmates, make a list of your *predictions* for the upcoming year.

G. Think Back

Answer the following questions according to the text.

1. Why would Lisa prefer to visit Florida in the winter?

2. What are some of Orlando's problems related to the establishment of Disney World nearby?

3. Why does Lisa describe the basement at Disney World as a nerve center?

4. Do you remember Lisa's statistics on Disney World? Match the numbers in column A with the letters in column B.

A	B
1. 2× Manhattan	a. basement
2. 717	b. campsites
3. 256	c. the Magic Kingdom
4. 8 acres	d. boats
5. 6 lands	e. Disney World

5. Why didn't Lisa follow her desire to become an astronaut?

H. Talk About It

1. What are typical motel rooms like in your native country? How are they similar to or different from the one Lisa describes?

2. Which of Walt Disney's characters and movies are you familiar with? Would you call Disney a genius? Why or why not?

3. The space program has always been a controversial issue in the United States because of the huge expenditures it requires. Do you feel that countries should go to this expense to explore space? Explain your answer with *valid* arguments.

I. Words, Words, Words!

The following vocabulary items have been taken from Lisa's article. Try to guess the meaning of each word from the context and write your definition in the space provided. When you have finished, check the vocabulary list at the end of the book for the correct meaning.

1. bar _____
Until women got the right to vote in 1920, they were *barred* from participating in elections.

2. brandish _____
The angry antinuclear demonstrator *brandished* a stick above his head.

3. contaminate _____
The oil refinery on the Gulf coast *contaminated* the air with smoke.

4. discrepancy _____
The Civil War, as Northerners call it, is referred to as the "War for Southern Independence" by Southerners—an interesting *discrepancy*.

5. discrimination _____
Many of the early settlers to the United States came to escape religious *discrimination* in their countries.

6. heightened _____

The popular Mardi Gras season in New Orleans is a period of *heightened* activity for city hotels and restaurants.

7. ineligible _____

United States citizens born in a foreign country are *ineligible* to run for the presidency of the United States, but can hold other important positions in the United States government.

8. persist _____

The cold weather *persisted* despite the weatherman's promise of warmer temperatures.

9. preach _____

Consumer advocate, Ralph Nader, *preaches* the need for consumers to be aware of the quality of products.

10. rare _____

Snowstorms are *rare* in Georgia where the climate is warm.

11. segregated _____

Some restaurants now have *segregated* seating arrangements for smokers and nonsmokers.

12. struggle _____

The United States' *struggle* for independence from Great Britain lasted from 1775 to 1783.

The early fighters for civil rights link arms and hopes in the 1963 March on Washington. The Reverend Martin Luther King is seventh from right.

"I HAVE A DREAM"

by Lisa Evans

1   Today in the South, blacks and whites work at the same jobs, live in the same neighborhoods, and attend the same schools. Interracial marriages, illegal in most southern states until 1967, are gradually increasing in number, although they are still rare. "Whites Only" signs have been removed from restaurants and other public places, and blacks are no longer barred from swimming pools because of fears that their black skin might contaminate the water.

2   It has taken a long time to achieve these steps toward racial equality. Blacks had been slaves in the South from 1619, when they were first brought to the New World by Dutch traders, until 1865 when the Civil War[1] finally freed them—a period of almost 250 years. White attitudes, however, were slow to respond to this change in the status of blacks, who continued to be treated as inferiors despite their emancipation.[2] It was not until almost a century later that blacks began to demand their rights as American citizens.

3   Many people feel the civil rights[3] movement started with a small incident in Montgomery, Alabama in 1955. On an unusually hot day in December, six whites boarded a Montgomery city bus. It was customary in the South for blacks to sit in the back of the bus, but on that particular day, seeing that the white section was full, the bus driver asked four black passengers in the rear to give their seats to the whites. Three of the blacks obeyed immediately, but the fourth, Rosa Parks, refused. She was subsequently arrested. Why didn't she move? As she later explained, she was simply tired from shopping and her feet hurt; she just didn't feel like standing. To protest her arrest, 50,000 Montgomery blacks boycotted the city bus system. They refused to ride on the buses until the company changed its policy of segregated seating. Since about 75 percent of the company's passengers had been blacks, the company lost a lot of money. The boycott continued for one year until the Supreme Court finally ruled that segregation on buses was illegal. The peaceful protest had succeeded.

4   The leader of the Montgomery bus boycott was a young black minister named Martin Luther King, Jr. During the next decade he was destined to become the most famous civil rights leader in the history of the United States. Dr. King believed that the struggle for equal rights should be peaceful, and he preached a philosophy of nonviolent resistance. In 1963 he led a march of more than 250,000 people, both white and black, in Washington, D.C., to demonstrate for equal rights. In his speech from the steps of the Lincoln Memorial, he spoke of his dream that someday people would "not be judged by the color of their skin but by the content of their character." In 1964, Martin Luther King, Jr., by then known throughout the world, received the Nobel prize for peace. Four years later, during a period of heightened racial tension, the peace-loving King was assassinated while attending a conference for civil rights in Memphis, Tennessee.

5   Under King's leadership, the early 1960s were characterized by peaceful protests, such as "sit-ins." At that time many restaurants and lunch counters in the South refused to serve blacks. In protest, blacks and sympathetic whites sat on stools at the counters of these restaurants and refused to move until they were served. These sit-ins were successful. Gradually, restaurants across the South were forced to abandon their policy of segregation.

6   During this period many of the more obvious signs of segregation disappeared as a result of nonviolent protests and federal legislation; however, the basic inequalities still existed. There were, for example, no longer separate drinking fountains and restrooms for blacks and whites, but racial discrimination remained widespread in jobs, schools, and elections. Employers refused to hire blacks for better positions, with the result that blacks were often forced to accept the most undesirable jobs. In many schools across the country, segregation continued despite the Supreme Court ruling that segregated schools were illegal because they did not provide children with equal educational opportunities. In addition, many blacks in the South were ineligible to vote because they could not meet the overly strict voting requirements established by whites in the southern states. Finally, in 1964, Congress passed the Civil Rights Act, probably the most important piece of legislation for minority groups in the United States. The law said that all Americans must be treated equally in regard to employment, education, the right to vote, and the use of public facilities. Equal rights for blacks were now at least a legal reality.

7   Nevertheless, tension in black communities continued to mount. Many blacks were frustrated by the slow progress which resulted from nonviolent protests and federal civil rights legislation. A new era, marked by nationwide racial violence, began in the mid-1960s. Between 1964 and 1968 there were 239 racially motivated riots across the country. Cities became battlefields with militant demonstrators shouting "Burn Baby Burn!" and police brandishing guns.

8   During this period blacks also developed a new pride in their race and history. They dropped the old term "Negro" in favor of "Afro-American" or "Black." Popular slogans such as "Black is beautiful" and "Black power" reflected their growing sense of unity and strength.

9   Racial tension decreased in the 1970s thanks to the gradual enforcement and acceptance of civil rights legislation. Today in the 1980s, despite the fact that blacks live in freedom and equality unparalleled in their American history, economic and social problems persist and incidents of racial discrimination and violence are not uncommon. A discrepancy still exists between legal rights and social realities. The true hope of the United States remains that someday Martin Luther King's dream will come true, " . . .that one day this nation will rise up and live out the true meaning of its creed:[4] 'We hold these truths to be self-evident, that all men are created equal.'"[5]

Notes

1. The Civil War: the war (1861–1865) between the northern (Union) and southern (Confederate) states in which slavery was a major issue.
2. emancipation: the act of freeing a person or people.

3. civil rights: the rights of all citizens to equal treatment in their country.
4. creed: belief.
5. Quote from the Declaration of Independence, adopted by Congress on July 4, 1776.

K. First Impressions

Do the following exercise without referring to the article. Circle the letter next to the statement that best answers the question.

1. Martin Luther King strongly believed in
   a. the need for violent demonstrations.
   b. peaceful protests.
   c. race riots.
   d. both a and c.

2. Which of the following is false? Interracial marriages are
   a. increasing.
   b. common.
   c. uncommon.
   d. legal.

3. In the United States, the latter half of the 1960s was a time of
   a. peaceful protests.
   b. segregated restaurants and public facilities.
   c. nonviolent resistance.
   d. violent demonstrations.

4. The Civil Rights Act of 1964 made racial discrimination illegal in
   a. employment.
   b. education.
   c. elections.
   d. the use of public facilities.
   e. all of the above.

5. The Montgomery bus boycott ended because
   a. the bus company lost a lot of money.
   b. the blacks needed the buses for transportation.
   c. the Supreme Court declared that segregation on buses was illegal.
   d. none of the above.

L. Rapid Reading

Do this exercise in class. Scan the article quickly to find the following pieces of information. Write down the number of the paragraph in which each topic is discussed.

a. _____ sit-ins

b. _____ black pride

c. _____ Martin Luther King's march in Washington, D.C.

d. _____ the Civil War

e. _____ race riots

f. _____ the Montgomery bus boycott

g. _____ the Civil Rights Act

M. Between the Lines

Circle the letter next to the statement that best answers the question. You may refer to the text.

1. Which of the following is the main idea of the article?
   a. Slavery in the South.
   b. The life of Martin Luther King, Jr.
   c. The civil rights movement in the United States.
   d. Peaceful protests succeed.

2. To "boycott" a company means
   a. to refuse to do business with it.
   b. to support its products.
   c. to compete with it.

3. In paragraph 7, sentence 1, the article states that tension continued to mount. In this context "mount" means
   a. to decrease.
   b. to increase.
   c. to get on a horse.
   d. to attach something to a surface.

4. In paragraph 2, sentence 3, "their" refers to
   a. attitudes.
   b. blacks.
   c. inferiors.
   d. whites.

5. The tone of the last paragraph is best described as
   a. somewhat hopeful.
   b. pessimistic.
   c. militant.
   d. overly optimistic.

N. More Expressions

Fill in the blanks with words from the following list. Use the correct voice, tense, and singular or plural form of the noun.

rare	segregated	discrepancy
discrimination	to contaminate	to persist
to preach	ineligible	struggle
	to bar	

1. Racially _____ public facilities were declared illegal by the Supreme Court.

2. Boat tours through the Everglades provide visitors with a close look at _____ birds, animals, and plants.

3. The Quakers, a religious group, _____ the evils of slavery in the 1800s.

4. The National Organization of Women (N.O.W.) is trying to eliminate sexual _____.

5. The _____ to rebuild the South after the Civil War took many years.

6. A(n) _____ existed between the number of people who had signed up for the course on Black History and the number who actually attended.

7. The majority of visitors at Disney World _____ from entering the park's "nerve center."

8. The student was _____ for a scholarship to Emory University in Atlanta because of his low grades.

9. Exhaust from automobile engines _____ the air with nitrogen oxides and carbon monoxide.

10. Hard feelings _____ between the North and the South for a long time after the Civil War had ended.

O. Express Yourself

1. Statistics show that women in the United States often earn lower salaries than men for the same jobs. Do you agree or disagree with this practice? How do you justify your answer?

2. Here are some *rarities*.
   People who enjoy paying income tax are *rare!*
   Snow in Florida is *rare!*
   E.S.L. students who love to take the TOEFL (Test of English as a Foreign Language) are *rare!*
   By yourself or with your classmates make a list of at least five types of people, places or things that are *rare*.

3. An unmarried man in the United States is sometimes referred to as an *eligible* bachelor. What do you think this means, and what makes him *eligible*?

P. Talk It Up

1. When were blacks first brought to the United States and by whom?

2. Why was Rosa Parks arrested?

3. What is a "sit-in"? What was one goal of sit-ins in the South?

4. There is an old saying, "Don't judge a book by its cover." How do those words relate to the beliefs held by Martin Luther King? In what ways can you apply that wisdom to experiences in your own life?

5. Many businesses and universities in the United States have a policy of affirmative action, that is, choosing a minority person for a position instead of a nonminority person who might be equally or more qualified in order to fill quotas for women, blacks, and other minorities. This practice has been called "reverse discrimination" by its opponents. What is your opinion of this practice?

Q. Word Families

Choose the appropriate form of the word. Be certain to use the correct verb tense, singular or plural form of the noun, and the passive voice where necessary.

1. (il)legality, to legalize, (il)legal, (il)legally
   a. _____ parked cars usually get a ticket and are sometimes towed away.
   b. It is _____ to shoot an alligator in the Everglades where animals are under the protection of the National Park Service.
   c. The _____ of marijuana does not prevent many people from using it.
   d. Many people would like _____ the drug.

2. ambition, ambitious, ambitiously
   a. Born in the music city of New Orleans, Louis (Satchmo) Armstrong was an _____ trumpet player.
   b. He worked _____ to perfect his technical and improvisational skills.
   c. His _____ was to become a leading jazz musician, and he succeeded.

3. resistance, to resist, resistant, irresistible
   a. Lisa could not _____ buying a bag of oranges when she was in Florida.
   b. The big, fresh grapefruit were also _____.
   c. Citrus fruit trees are not _____ to extremely cold temperatures.
   d. Because of this low _____ to cold, they can be seriously damaged when temperatures drop below freezing.

4. discrimination, to discriminate, discriminatory
   a. Laws have been passed making _____ in employment illegal.
   b. An employer who _____ against an employee on the basis of race, religion, or sex may be taken to court.
   c. Unfortunately, such _____ practices often go unnoticed.

5. persistence, to persist, persistent, persistently
   a. The _____ of Abraham Lincoln and other antislavery advocates led to the end of slavery in America.
   b. Henry Ford was a _____ individual who built one of America's largest industries.
   c. In spite of the public's resistance to his "horseless carriage," Ford _____ in building his new cars.
   d. You will learn to speak perfect English if you study _____.

6. contamination, contaminant, to contaminate, contaminated
   a. _____ from oil spills is a serious problem in the Gulf of Mexico.
   b. _____ water can kill fish.
   c. Companies that _____ the environment may have to pay large fines.
   d. _____ in the water and air can create serious health hazards.

7. validity, to validate, valid, invalid
   a. A driver's license is not _____ until it is signed by the bearer.
   b. Steve was surprised to discover that his driver's license was _____; it had expired the previous week.
   c. The antinuclear group questioned the _____ of building a new nuclear power plant in Georgia.
   d. The power company _____ its claim by providing statistics showing a need for the facility.

8. fantasy, to fantasize, fantastic, fantastically
   a. For people interested in scuba diving, the Florida Keys are a _____ vacation spot.
   b. The water around the islands is _____ clear, giving underwater swimmers a great view of fish and rock formations.
   c. When Lisa was nine years old she _____ about being an astronaut.
   d. Her favorite _____ included traveling to the moon with a pet monkey.

9. amusement, to amuse, amusing, amused
   a. Lisa's favorite form of _____ while traveling was singing along with the radio.
   b. Walt Disney's movies and cartoons _____ children and grown-ups since 1926.
   c. His _____ stories include such lovable characters as Mickey Mouse, Goofy, and Cinderella.
   d. The _____ children clapped loudly after the Mickey Mouse cartoon.

10. specifications, to specify, specific, specifically
   a. When the Apollo capsule flew to the moon, the astronauts' instructions _____ the correct procedure to follow for the landing.
   b. The space program has strict requirements for its astronauts, _____, that they be in excellent physical and mental health.
   c. The ground control knows the _____ time and place the capsule will touch down on earth.

d. The _____ for rockets at Cape Canaveral are in the metric system.

R. Look It Up

1. In the mid-1800s the term "Underground Railroad" did not refer to a subway. What was the "Underground Railroad"?

2. What is a "carpetbagger"?

3. What are the "Orange Bowl" and the "Sugar Bowl"?

4. "Oh, I wish I were in Dixie," is a line from a well-known folk song written in 1859. Where is "Dixie" and what type of music is particularly common in New Orleans?

CANADA
U.S.A.

1.
Lake Superior

MINNESOTA

CANADA

Cu   Fe   Cu

Fe
M
Fe
I
C
H
DAIRY   I
WISCONSIN   G   Lake Huron
A
DAIRY   N   G

Madison   Lake Michigan   Sugarbeets
DAIRY   Lansing ★   CANADA
Milwaukee   DAIRY   Detroit   Lake Erie   NEW
(Beer)   (Cars)   YORK

IOWA   Galena   V   U.S.A.   PENN.

Chicago   S   O   V   Cleveland
DAIRY   DAIRY
S
O   V   G
S   Fort
Wayne   OHIO
C
ILLINOIS   INDIANA   S
C
★ Springfield   C   Columbus   Ri
C   S   O   Indianapolis   Cincinnati   O   C
MISSOURI   S   O   C   Ohio   WEST VIRGINIA
C   S   C
S
C   River
Ohio   KENTUCKY

MILES
0   50   100   150

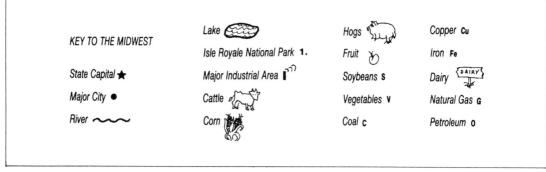

KEY TO THE MIDWEST   Lake   Hogs   Copper Cu

Isle Royale National Park 1.   Fruit   Iron Fe

State Capital ★   Major Industrial Area   Soybeans S   Dairy DAIRY

Major City ●   Cattle   Vegetables V   Natural Gas G

River   Corn   Coal C   Petroleum O

chapter 5

The Midwest

A. Take a Look

I. Answer the following questions by looking at the map:

1. Which is the major dairy state?

2. Which are the major corn producing states?

3. Which state(s) touch(es) four of the five Great Lakes?

4. Where are sugar beets grown?

5. Which state capital includes its state in its name?

6. Which city makes a popular beverage in the United States?

II. Make up questions that could be answered by the following information:

1. Illinois, Michigan, Ohio, Kentucky

2. The Ohio River

3. Iron and copper

4. Madison

5. Along the eastern shore of Lake Michigan

B. A Letter from Lisa

Galena, Illinois
July 5

Dear Steve,

It was a long trip from Florida to Illinois. I drove straight through, stopping only to eat and sleep, so I didn't have much of a chance to write. I promise, however, that my articles for the <u>Daily</u> will continue to be in on time.

I stopped for a day to visit Chicago, the "Windy City," and it <u>is</u> windy! The breeze from Lake Michigan feels wonderful on a hot July afternoon, but it must be terrible in January. I bet a lot of people in Chicago head for Florida in the winter.

You know, I got to Chicago just in time. After driving through all those inland states, I was beginning to miss the ocean. When I saw Lake Michigan, I immediately felt a lot better. It seemed impossible that it was only a lake. There were huge freighters and yachts,[1] and sandy beaches covered with people. If I hadn't known I was in Illinois, I would have sworn I was looking at the Atlantic. It's obvious how the Great Lakes got their name!

Anyway, I was at a gas station in Chicago, and the attendant, noticing my suitcase and typewriter in the back seat, asked me where I was going. After I had explained briefly, he recommended that I visit his hometown, Galena. Being a reporter, I couldn't resist a "hot tip,"[2] so I decided to take his advice.

The drive to Galena was pleasant enough. First I passed through flat farm country with fields of corn and soybeans—part of the famous Corn Belt.[3] Then, just east of Galena, the land suddenly became hilly, and I found myself driving along the top of a high ridge from which I had a glorious view of charming little farms and forested hills. Apparently the glaciers missed this small area of the Midwest, which explains the abrupt change from flat land to rolling hills and rocky bluffs.[4]

It's hard to imagine that the sleepy little town of Galena was once one of the major commercial centers of the Upper Mississippi. In the first half of the nineteenth century, owners of lead mines, steamboat captains, and enterprising traders were making huge fortunes in Galena, but the town's days of prosperity were numbered. First, the railroad came along and gradually replaced the steamboat; then the lead mines closed, and finally, the Galena River filled with mud. What's that old expression? "Bad luck always comes in threes," I think.

Today, though, instead of the ghost town[5] you might expect to find under those circumstances, Galena is still very much alive. The town's sources of prosperity have disappeared, but the beautiful homes, built on the hills on either side of the river during Galena's heyday, have remained virtually intact. In fact, the whole town has a quaint, old-world charm that I find fascinating. I also went to a few of Galena's museums to get a better idea of life in the Midwest of the 1800s.

You know, I'm impressed. Galena is an excellent example of how a town can tastefully exploit its history to guarantee its future economic stability.

Speaking of taste, I had the good fortune to arrive on Sunday, just in time for Galena's annual ice cream social. I've never seen, or tasted, so many kinds of delicious, homemade ice cream, including my favorite, peach. By the time I spotted the huge assortment of cakes and pies, also homemade by the townspeople, I couldn't eat another thing! Ugh! I <u>did</u> consider bringing you a quart of ice cream as a souvenir, Steve, but I was afraid it would melt.

Today I drove to Warren for the county fair where I inspected the prizewinning cows, pigs, and sheep. The 4H[6] clubs are really big[7] out here in the Midwest, and many farm children spend months preparing their special animals for fair competition. I have to admit, though, that what I enjoyed most were the vegetables. Now, I'm not a vegetable fan, but even I was impressed by the blue-ribboned[8] "biggest ear of corn," "the fattest tomato," and "the largest pumpkin." I never knew vegetables could grow to such proportions! I was also amazed by the array of fruit preserves[9] and canned vegetables. People around here take their gardening seriously and like to "save a bit of summer in a jar" for those cold winter months.

Before returning to Galena, I spent a few hours walking down the midway[10] with all the games, rides, and colored lights. What good, old-fashioned fun! I'd rather take a ride on a roller coaster[11] than play a video computer game any day!

Well, tomorrow I head west again. I plan to stop in Dubuque, Iowa for a ride on an old Mississippi paddlewheeler, and from there, I'm off to Iowa City where I pick up I-80[12] for Kansas.

Take care,

Lisa

P.S. Did you know that <u>nine</u> union generals in the Civil War came from Galena? One of them was Ulysses S. Grant, eighteenth President of the United States.

Notes

1. freighters and yachts: large ships for carrying goods and large pleasure boats.
2. "hot tip": (slang) some excellent advice from one supposedly having special knowledge on a subject.
3. Corn Belt: an area in the United States extending from Ohio to Nebraska, especially suited for growing corn.
4. bluff: a high, steep hill with a flat top.
5. ghost town: a once prosperous town, now abandoned.
6. 4H stands for "head, heart, hands, and health." A program set up by the United States Department of Agriculture to teach children skills for the home and farm as well as good citizenship.

7. big: (slang) popular.
8. blue ribbon: awarded for first place in a competition.
9. preserves: fruit which has been canned or made into jams or jellies.
10. midway: an avenue at a fair with rides and games of skill and luck.
11. roller coaster: an elevated railway in an amusement park made with curves and hills on which the cars roll.
12. I-80: the major east-west interstate highway extending from New York to San Francisco.

C. True or False?

Write T before those statements that are true and F before those that are false.

_____ 1. Lisa thought Lake Michigan resembled an ocean.

_____ 2. Today, Galena is best known for its museums and nineteenth century homes.

_____ 3. Lisa loves to eat vegetables and, consequently, really enjoyed the vegetable competition at the county fair.

_____ 4. Galena's decline in prosperity can be attributed in part to the arrival of the railroad.

_____ 5. The drive from Florida to Illinois took a long time because Lisa stopped often.

_____ 6. When glaciers covered the land surrounding Galena, they made hills and rocky bluffs.

_____ 7. Once a year, the townspeople of Galena hold an ice cream social.

_____ 8. Lisa filled up with cake and ice cream at the Galena social.

_____ 9. Galena was the site of an important battle in the Civil War.

_____ 10. A county fair is a fun place to be if you like animals, vegetables, and amusement parks.

D. Close-up

Fill in the blanks with a, an, or the. If no article is necessary, put an X in the blank.

Lisa, _____ enthusiastic antique doll collector, was delighted to learn that
(1)

_____ Galena's Main Street, also known as "_____ Wall," was filled
(2)   (3)

with _____ antique shops. While walking along _____ curving street,
(4)   (5)

and looking at all _____ window displays, Lisa spotted _____ antique
(6)   (7)

porcelain doll from _____ Victorian era. _____ owner of this particular
        (8)   (9)

shop was _____ friendly old man who had been selling _____ antiques
         (10)   (11)

for more than _____ four decades. He and Lisa talked for _____ few
              (12)   (13)

minutes while she examined _____ doll. Then, convinced that it was
                            (14)

really _____ antique and not just _____ good copy, Lisa bought herself
       (15)   (16)

_____ new traveling companion!
 (17)

E. Expressions

Rewrite the following sentences, replacing the italicized words with the correct form of the appropriate word or expression.

to swear	abrupt	intact
quaint	to exploit	heyday
fan	circumstances	prosperity
	virtually	

1. After speeding up and down hills and around curves, the roller coaster finally came to a *sudden* stop at the end of the track.

2. Although Indians and French explorers had discovered and mined the lead deposits in the Galena area, it wasn't until the beginning of the nineteenth century that the United States started *to take advantage of* this mineral wealth.

3. Pigs are most often pictured as being very dirty, but those Lisa saw at the county fair were *almost entirely* spotless!

4. Considering the *conditions* of the past week, Lisa was not very surprised to discover that she had gained ten pounds.

5. Much of Chicago's *economic well-being* is due to its huge meat-packing industry.

6. In spite of the bumpy back roads that bounced Mrs. Owens and the contents of her pick-up truck all around, her tasty peach pie arrived *in one piece* for the competition at the county fair.

7. Wilbur Jones *had stated in all seriousness* that he would win a blue ribbon at the county fair; however, people didn't believe him until he arrived in Warren with a pumpkin so big that he needed help carrying it!

8. Even though Lisa knew Steve was an *enthusiastic admirer* of the Boston Red Sox, she still bought a Chicago White Sox pennant for him as a souvenir.

9. Lisa found Galena to be a mixture of modern ideas and *old-fashioned* charm.

10. Paddlewheelers had their *period of greatest use* in the nineteenth century. Now they serve only as tourist attractions.

F. Express Yourself

1. *To exploit* can also have negative connotations. Think of contexts where it might be used negatively.

2. Are you a *fan* of someone or something? Share your enthusiasm with your classmates.

3. People sometimes say that a certain person has an *abrupt* manner. What do you think *abrupt* means when it's used to describe a person?

G. Think Back

Answer the following questions according to the text.

1. What did Lake Michigan remind Lisa of and why?

2. Name some of the activities found at a county fair.

3. How did glaciers shape the land around Chicago and Galena?

4. Name three reasons why Galena was prosperous during the nineteenth century, and then name the three factors that led to Galena's decline as a major commercial center.

5. Why was Lisa impressed with the town of Galena?

H. Talk About It

1. Do you have any special programs for children in your native country which are similar to 4H? If so, what are they?

2. County fairs are important social events all over rural America. Do you have similar events in your native country? How are they similar? How are they different?

3. Lisa grew up near the ocean and prefers to live on the coast, so she would find it difficult to live inland. Do you live inland or on a coast, and would you also find it difficult to switch? If so, what would you miss?

I. Words, Words, Words!

The following vocabulary items have been taken from Lisa's article. Try to guess the meaning of each word from the context and write your definition in the space provided. When you have finished, check the vocabulary list at the end of the book for the correct meaning.

1. compensate _____
   Lisa *compensated* for having missed lunch by eating a big dinner before going to the ice cream social.

2. defect _____
   The new car had to be sent back to its factory in Detroit because of a *defect* in the engine.

3. deplete _____
   By spring the family had almost *depleted* their supply of canned tomatoes and green beans from the previous summer.

4. devastating _____
   The heavy rains and high winds were *devastating* for the farmer's crops.

5. feat _____
   Winning the Indianapolis 500, one of the most famous auto races in the world, is a *feat* which requires great skill and effort.

6. flourish _____
   The town of Galena *flourished* during its heyday in the nineteenth century.

7. innovation _____
   The tractor was an *innovation* that completely changed farming practices.

8. keep up with _____
   The 4H clubs help farm children *keep up with* the latest farming techniques.

9. offspring _____

The *offspring* of the grand champion bull won many prizes at the county fair.

10. remarkable _____

Lisa thought that it was *remarkable* how big Lake Michigan was.

11. replenish _____

The rain storm *replenished* the town's water supply which had gotten low.

12. reserve _____

A large *reserve* of iron ore is located in northern Michigan.

13. sustain _____

Having had three dishes of ice cream, Lisa could no longer *sustain* her enthusiasm for eating.

14. trait _____

Lisa had inherited several of her father's *traits,* including his blue eyes and brown hair.

15. undergo _____

The American automobile has *undergone* many changes during the past ten years; for example, cars are now smaller and more fuel-efficient.

Dairy cattle grazing on a Midwestern farm.

(Courtesy USDA-SCS. Photo by Erwin W. Cole)

J. Headline

KEEPING FOOD ON THE TABLE

by Lisa Evans

1   It's early August and the countryside appears peaceful. Planting has long been finished and the fields are alive with strong, healthy crops. Soybeans and wheat are flourishing under the hot summer sun, and the corn, which was "knee-high by the fourth of July," is now well over six feet tall. Herds of dairy and beef cattle are grazing[1] peacefully in rolling pastures which surround big, red barns and neat, white farmhouses. Everything as far as the eye can see radiates a sense of prosperity. Welcome to the Midwest—one of the most fertile agricultural regions of the world.

2   The tranquility of the above scene is misleading. Farmers in the Midwest put in some of the longest workdays of any profession in the United States. In addition to caring for their crops and livestock, they have to keep up with new farming techniques, such as those for combating soil erosion and increasing livestock production. It is essential that farmers adopt these advances in technology if they want to continue to meet the growing demands of a hungry world.

3   Agriculture is the number one industry in the United States and agricultural products are the country's leading export. American farmers manage to feed not only the total population of the United States, but also millions of other people throughout the rest of the world. Corn and soybean exports alone account for approximately 75 percent of the amount sold in world markets.

4   This productivity, however, has its price. Intensive cultivation exposes the earth to the damaging forces of nature. Every year wind and water remove tons of rich soil from the nation's croplands, with the result that soil erosion has become a national problem concerning everyone from the farmer to the consumer.

5   Each field is covered by a limited amount of topsoil, the upper layer of earth which is richest in the nutrients and minerals necessary for growing crops. Ever since the first farmers arrived in the Midwest almost 200 years ago, cultivation and, consequently, erosion have been depleting the supply of topsoil. In the 1830s, nearly two feet of rich, black topsoil covered the Midwest. Today the average depth is only eight inches, and every decade another inch is blown or washed away. This erosion is steadily decreasing the productivity of valuable cropland. A United States Agricultural Department survey states that if erosion continues at its present rate, corn and soybean yields[2] in the Midwest may drop as much as 30 percent over the next 50 years.

6   So far, farmers have been able to compensate for the loss of fertile topsoil by applying more chemical fertilizers to their fields; however, while this practice has increased crop yields, it has been devastating for ecology. Agriculture has become one of the biggest polluters of the nation's precious water supply. Rivers, lakes, and underground reserves of water are being filled in and poisoned by soil and chemicals carried by drainage[3] from eroding fields. Furthermore, fertilizers only replenish the soil; they do not prevent its loss.

7   Clearly something else has to be done in order to avoid an eventual ecological disaster. Conservationists insist that the solution to the problem lies in new and better farming techniques. Concerned farmers are building terraces on hilly fields, rotating their crops, and using new plowing methods to cut soil losses significantly. Substantial progress has been made, but soil erosion is far from being under control.

8   The problems and innovations of the agricultural industry in the Midwest are not restricted to growing crops. Livestock raising, which is big business in the central region of the United States, is also undergoing many changes. Recent developments in technology have enabled farmers to raise not only healthier animals, but more animals as well. By employing the techniques of superovulation, artificial insemination, and embryo transfer, farmers can more than triple the number of offspring produced by a single cow per year.

9   The procedure for accomplishing this remarkable feat is as follows. First, the farmer chooses a cow on the basis of certain valuable traits, such as rapid weight gain or high milk production. A veterinarian then injects the cow with hormones which cause the animal to superovulate, that is, to produce more eggs, or "ova," than the usual one or two. As many as ten or more ova may be released in one superovulation.

10   While the ova are moving down the Fallopian tubes toward the uterus,[4] about five days after superovulation, the cow is artificially inseminated with semen from a prize bull. If the insemination is successful, the eggs are fertilized and become living embryos, each of which has the potential to develop into a calf.

11   Next comes the process of embryo transfer. After the embryos have developed in the uterus for six to eight days, they are carefully removed and examined for defects. Each healthy embryo is then implanted in the uterus of a *different* cow, where it continues to develop. Nine months later the surrogate[5] mother gives birth to a healthy calf to which she is not genetically related.

12   The result of the entire procedure is that a farmer can increase the size of a herd of cows at a rate which was previously impossible. Although three to four calves are the average, as many as ten or more may be produced from the embryos of one mother cow. The possible applications of these techniques are overwhelming when one considers that by freezing an embryo until its sister embryo has been born and become sexually mature, it is even possible for a cow to give birth to its identical twin sister!

13   As the world's population continues to increase, farmers will be called upon to produce more and more life-sustaining food. Constant technological advances in soil conservation and livestock production will be required to keep pace with this ever-growing need. One concern, however, is that while this technology is solving old problems, it may be creating new ones in the process.

Notes

1. graze: to eat grass.
2. yield: harvest.
3. drainage: the flow of excess water.

4. uterus: the organ of the female that contains the young during development before birth.
5. surrogate: something that serves as a substitute.

K. First Impressions

*Do the following exercise without referring to the article. Circle the letter next to the
statement that best answers the question.*

1. According to the article, agriculture in the United States is
   a. the number one industry.
   b. the second largest source of exports.
   c. the number one source of exports.
   d. second only to the automobile industry.
   e. both a and c.

2. In order to compensate for the loss of topsoil, farmers have been
   a. using new plowing methods.
   b. building artificial lakes on their farms.
   c. planting less corn.
   d. putting fertilizers on their fields.
   e. both a and d.

3. According to the article, the solution to the problem of soil erosion lies in
   a. better farming methods.
   b. the use of fertilizers.
   c. increased cultivation.
   d. new types of plant seed.

4. Which procedure occurs first in the series?
   a. Artificial insemination.
   b. Superovulation.
   c. The birth of a calf.
   d. Embryo transfer.

5. Which of the following is true?
   a. Embryos are unfertilized eggs.
   b. Soil erosion is almost under control.
   c. Embryo transfer is a process used to increase calf production.
   d. Erosion is caused only by water.

L. Rapid Reading

*Do this exercise in class. Scan the article quickly to find the following pieces of infor-
mation. Write down the number of the paragraph in which each topic is discussed.*

a. _____ artificial insemination

b. _____ new farming techniques

c. _____ agricultural exports

d. _____ embryo transfer

e. _____ the steady loss of topsoil

f. _____ water pollution from fertilizers

g. _____ superovulation

M. Between the Lines

Circle the letter next to the statement that best answers the question. You may refer to the text.

1. The main idea of the article is:
   a. Soil conservation methods are necessary to maintain high crop yields.
   b. New techniques for increasing livestock production are required to feed the world's population.
   c. Midwestern farmers are involved in both livestock raising and crop production.
   d. Farmers must adopt new advances in technology if they want to feed the world's population.

2. In paragraph 7, the article states that substantial progress has been made. In this context "progress" is pronounced
   a. pro' gress.
   b. pro gress'.

3. When an animal "superovulates," it produces
   a. an extremely large egg.
   b. more than the usual number of eggs.
   c. no eggs at all.

4. In paragraph 11, sentence 3, "it" refers to
   a. the embryos.
   b. the uterus.
   c. the cow.
   d. the embryo.

5. Paragraph 13 implies that
   a. the world's food needs are decreasing.
   b. soil and water conservation are not important.
   c. the process of embryo transfer may cause problems in the future.
   d. progress is always for the good of society.

N. More Expressions

Fill in the blanks with words from the following list. Use the correct voice, tense, and singular or plural form of the noun.

to compensate   trait   innovation
to deplete   defect   to replenish
devastating   to sustain   to keep up with
                remarkable

1. Abraham Lincoln's honesty and dependability were two of his best

   _____.

2. The assembly line was one of Henry Ford's _____ which revolutionized industry in the early twentieth century.

3. Sudden storms on Lake Superior, the largest freshwater lake in the world, can be _____ for small fishing boats.

4. Driving straight through from Florida to Chicago _____ Lisa's supply of energy.

5. The _____ number of airplanes that fly into and out of Chicago's O'Hare airport has made it one of the busiest airports in the world.

6. It was difficult for Lisa _____ the news from Boston while she was traveling.

7. The Cleveland Symphony _____ its place among the top American orchestras for many years.

8. The interesting people and places Lisa had visited on her trip
_____ for being away from family and friends.

9. At a restaurant along the highway, Lisa _____ the
thermos of coffee that she kept in the car.

10. Having listened to the politician's speech, Lisa felt there were several
_____ in his argument.

O. Express Yourself

1. Which of your *traits* did you inherit from your mother? Which came from your father?

2. What are some of the most *remarkable* differences between your native country and the United States? In what ways are the two countries *remarkably* similar?

3. How do you manage *to keep up with* the news from home when you are away? Do you think it is important for people *to keep up with* national and world politics? Why or why not?

P. Talk It Up

1. What is topsoil?

2. What effect do fertilizers have on fields? On the water supply?

3. Explain how a farmer can triple the number of offspring produced by a single cow.

4. How can a cow give birth to its twin sister?

5. These new technological developments in the cattle industry have led to significant advances in human medicine. Several "test-tube" babies have already been born to parents around the world. How do you feel about this?

6. Science has already enabled farmers to produce genetically superior offspring. Many people fear that these and other techniques used in genetic research may be misused; they feel that government control is necessary. Should the federal government make laws restricting such research?

Q. Word Families

Choose the appropriate form of the word. Be certain to use the correct verb tense, singular or plural form of the noun, and the passive voice where necessary.

1. prosperity, to prosper, prosperous
   a. Business was slow during the winter, but in the summer the ice cream shop _____.
   b. The opening of the new factory brought back _____to the small Indiana town.
   c. The _____ farmer bought a new tractor in preparation for spring planting.

2. production, productivity, product, to produce, productive, productively
   a. Several manufacturers of rubber _____ are located in Akron, Ohio, the "Rubber Capital of the World."
   b. Pork _____ has increased due to advances in hog nutrition.
   c. Every year the Corn Belt also _____ more hogs than any other section of the country.
   d. The field's _____ improved after the farmer applied fertilizer.
   e. During the busy spring planting season, the farmer worked _____ late into the night.
   f. It was a _____ summer; corn and soybean yields exceeded those of the previous year.

3. compensation, to compensate
   a. Workers in the automobile industry, as in other industries, receive monetary _____ for working overtime.
   b. Unions make certain that employees _____ fairly for the extra hours they put in.

4. depletion, to deplete
   a. The rapid _____ of Michigan's forests brought an end to the state's great lumber industry.
   b. _____ our natural resources is to ignore our future.

5. devastation, to devastate, devastating, devastated
   a. Several cities along the Ohio River _____ by a terrible flood last spring.
   b. The _____ flood waters ruined homes and businesses.
   c. The President of the United States came to view the _____.
   d. The _____ cities were eligible for aid from the United States government to help repair the damage.

6. taste, to taste, tasty, tasteful, tasteless, tastefully
   a. When she was in Galena, Lisa had a _____ meal at an old country inn.
   b. There she _____ some of local specialties, including steak and sweet corn.
   c. Everything was delicious except for the potatoes which were _____.
   d. The attractive dining room of the inn had been _____ redecorated in various shades of blue.
   e. _____ bouquets of flowers brightened the room.
   f. The owner of the inn obviously had good _____.

7. progress, progression, to progress, progressive, progressively
   a. Cars _____ rapidly along assembly lines in Detroit factories.
   b. Over the years, American cars have gotten _____ smaller and more efficient.
   c. Considerable _____ has been made toward decreasing the amount of pollutants in car exhaust.
   d. A steady _____ of technological improvements has led to a computer-controlled automobile engine.
   e. American automobile manufacturers have had to become more _____ to compete with foreign companies.

8. substance, to substantiate, substantial, substantially
   a. Wisconsin, "America's Dairyland," produces a _____ amount of the cheese and other dairy products consumed in the United States.
   b. _____ have been added to cattle feed to improve beef production.
   c. Experience at the gas pump _____ the claim that new American cars get better gas mileage.
   d. Extensive mining of lead and coal has _____ depleted the mineral resources of Illinois and other Midwestern states.

9. remark, to remark, remarkable, remarkably
   a. Lisa did not hear the _____ made by the guide at Chicago's Museum of Science and Industry.
   b. Visitors to Isle Royal National Park in Lake Superior always _____ on the island's beauty and serenity.
   c. The construction of many skyscrapers has produced a _____ change in the Chicago skyline.
   d. The water of the Great Lakes is _____ cold even during the hot summer months.

10. charm, to charm, charming, charmingly
    a. Lisa _____ by the friendliness of the people she met in the Midwest.

b. Many of the beautiful, nineteenth century homes in Galena are
_____ decorated with pieces of furniture typical of that
era.

c. Mackinac Island is a _____ resort located between
Michigan's upper and lower peninsulas.

d. The _____ of the island is heightened by the absence of
motorized vehicles.

R. Look It Up

1. What are the names of the five Great Lakes?

2. Who was Al Capone?

3. What did Mrs. O'Leary's cow supposedly have to do with the Great
Chicago Fire of 1871?

4. Could a Hoosier carry a Buckeye in his pocket?

5. Henry Ford played a significant role in developing industry in the United
States. Look up some information on the founder of Ford Motor Company.

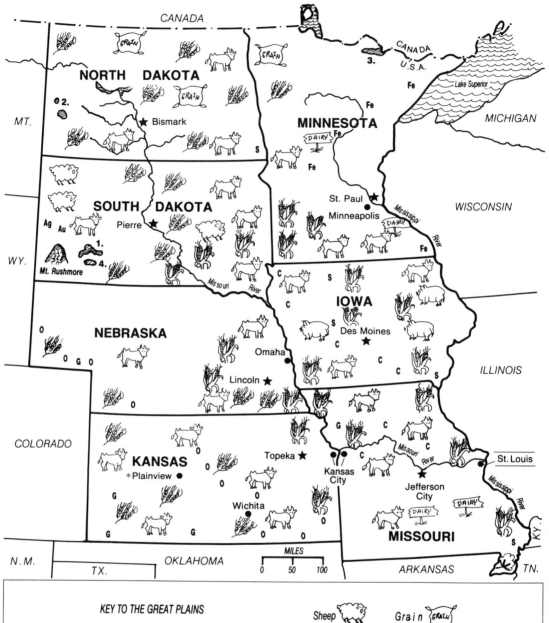

CANADA

NORTH DAKOTA

GRAIN

GRAIN

Ⓞ 2.

MT.

★ Bismark

GRAIN

CANADA
U.S.A.
3.

Fe

Fe

Lake Superior

MICHIGAN

MINNESOTA

Fe

DAIRY Fe

Fe

SOUTH DAKOTA

Pierre ★

St. Paul
Minneapolis

WISCONSIN

Ag Au

1.

4.

Mt. Rushmore

Mississippi River

DAIRY

Fe

WY.

Missouri River

NEBRASKA

O

O G O

Omaha

Lincoln ★

IOWA

C

C

S

S

C

Des Moines ★

C

S

ILLINOIS

COLORADO

O

KANSAS

*Plainview ●

Topeka ★

O

O

G

G

G

Wichita ●

O

O

G

C

Kansas City

C

Missouri River

Jefferson City ★

St. Louis

Mississippi River

DAIRY

DAIRY

MISSOURI

S

KY.

N.M.

TX.

OKLAHOMA

MILES

0   50   100

ARKANSAS

TN.

KEY TO THE GREAT PLAINS

State Capital ★

Major City ●

River ~~~ Lake 🥐

Badlands National Park **1.**

Theodore Roosevelt National Park **2.**

Voyageurs National Park **3.**

Wind Cave National Park **4.**

Cattle

Sheep

Hogs

Soybeans **S**

Corn

Wheat

Grain GRAIN

Dairy DAIRY   Cotton

Gold **Au**   Silver **Ag**

Iron **Fe**   Coal **C**

Natural Gas **G**   Petroleum **O**

chapter 6

The Great Plains

A. Take a Look

I. Answer the following questions by looking at the map:

1. How many states border on Missouri?
2. Where are large iron deposits located?
3. Where is the source of the Mississippi River?
4. Which are the major wheat producing states?
5. Which state has precious minerals?
6. Which two cities were named after presidents?

II. Make up questions that could be answered by the following information:

1. Bismarck
2. Cattle
3. Nebraska, Missouri, Colorado, and Oklahoma
4. Canada
5. St. Louis

Plain View is a fictitious but typical town of the Great Plains.

B. A Letter from Lisa

Plain View, Kansas
July 10

Dear Steve,

There I was, driving along Interstate 70 through western Kansas on my way to New Mexico when I saw a sign that made me slam on my brakes[1]—"Plain View, population 606, next right." What a coincidence! My Grandma and Grandpa Evans used to own a farm in Plain View, Kansas until 1935 when they sold everything and moved east. I can remember, as a little girl, listening to all sorts of stories they used to tell about their life in Kansas. I loved hearing about the different animals they raised on the farm, but I used to be terrified by their stories of the suffocating dust[2] storms of the 1930s. As a child, I had no real idea of what had happened—of how the dust destroyed the fields and just about ruined the regional economy, which, of course, was already crippled by the Depression.[3] I do remember, though, vividly picturing the dust from the barren, dry fields blowing into Grandma and Grandpa's house through tightly closed doors and windows and covering everything, even their dinner while they were eating. I could also imagine what it was like to be in the middle of a dust storm and not be able to see more than a foot in front of me. When I saw the sign for Plain View, all these stories came back to me, and I wanted to see where everything had taken place.

To be quite honest, now that I'm here, I find it almost impossible to believe those dust storm stories. Everywhere I look there are endless fields of tall, golden yellow wheat. It's obvious why the Great Plains are called "the breadbasket of America." And what a horizon! There are no hills or apartment buildings to block my view—just the endless, flat, open spaces of the plains with an occasional windmill or silo[4] high above the fields. Having spent so much time in the congested streets of Boston, I am overwhelmed by the vastness of the countryside here.

I'm staying in a little boarding house where I became friends with the owner who, believe it or not, actually remembers my grandparents! While I was sharing my impressions of the plains with her, she surprised me by insisting that she couldn't imagine how I could enjoy living in the city with "all those big buildings blocking the view." It is true that we're all more comfortable in the physical environment we're accustomed to. Having grown up in New England, it's hard for me to imagine living in a place with no trees, and I told her so. "Well," she answered, "there are a few trees, you know. Some grow naturally along the streams, and others are planted by farmers to protect their farms from the wind. And then, too, some individuals just plant one or two to decorate their lawns or to observe Arbor Day.[5] Now that's a really important holiday out here on the prairie!"

This morning I drove out to what used to be Grandma and Grandpa's farm. It's part of an enormous beef cattle ranch now, run by a Mr. Baker, who was very friendly and offered to show me around. Everything, of course, was totally automated. Imagine, Mr. Baker presses a button and immediately a machine in the cattle barn not only carries feed to thousands of hungry cattle, but also balances its fat and protein content! Obviously, the computer age has come to the farming and ranching industries.

According to Mr. Baker, though, in spite of all the fancy equipment, the fact is that nature still has the upper hand here. Everyone depends on the rain, but only nature can make it fall. Nature is also responsible for the violent windstorms. Twisters are a part of life on the plains, but you don't always know when to expect them. In fact, the only thing predictable about them is their unpredictability! Mr. Baker told me he once wrote a letter to a friend who lived 80 miles away. Before he could mail it a tornado hit town. The very next day, Mr. Baker's friend found the letter on his front lawn—no stamp was necessary. That's what I'd call "special delivery"! Mr. Baker said he also knew a man who went to bed during a twister and woke up on the floor the next morning wearing his pajamas inside out and backwards!

All kidding aside, I'm going to suggest to my grandparents that they come see how much life has changed around here since they left. Everything is done on a huge scale nowadays—no more little farms. But in spite of all the changes, my impression is that the people are still very much the same as Grandpa and Grandma described them—direct, honest, simple, and hardworking.

Speaking of hardworking, I'd better get back in my car and start driving. It's a long way to Santa Fe.

Take care. Love to all,

Lisa

P.S. I'm sending you a T-shirt I picked up at the University of Iowa. It reads "University of Iowa, Idaho City, Ohio." I think someone's trying to confuse people from the East Coast!

Notes

1. to slam on one's brake: to stop suddenly.
2. dust: fine, dry dirt.
3. The Great Depression: a period in the 1930s characterized by extremely low economic activity and a high rate of unemployment.
4. silo: a tall, sealed, cylindrical building used for making and storing animal feed.
5. Arbor Day: a holiday designated for planting trees.

C. True or False?

Write T before those statements which are true and F before those which are false.

      1. Lisa had planned on stopping in Plain View.

      2. Lisa didn't entirely believe Mr. Baker's stories about the twisters.

      3. According to Mr. Baker, modern technology hasn't conquered nature yet.

      4. Only tightly closed windows and doors could stop the dust from coming in during the dust storms.

      5. The 1930s were catastrophic for the Great Plains region.

      6. The only trees in the Plain View area are those that man has planted.

      7. The University of Iowa is located in Ohio.

      8. Lisa's grandparents are related to the owner of the boarding house.

      9. Lisa felt that although the lifestyle in Plain View had changed, the people were still much the same as before.

      10. Lisa felt that computers would soon be used on the farms and ranches of the Great Plains.

D. Close-up

Fill in the blanks with the appropriate prepositions.

_____ (1) 1934, Grandma and Grandpa Evans were still living _____ (2) a farm just outside _____ (3) Plain View, Kansas. This, _____ (4) course, was _____ (5) the Depression when there were not a lot _____ (6) jobs and the economy _____ (7) the United States, _____ (8) general, was very bad.

_____ (9) 1935, they became fed up _____ (10) farming, so they sold their house and land _____ (11) a modest sum _____ (12) money and moved _____ (13) Boston. Until Lisa's letter came, they had never thought _____ (14) returning

_____ Kansas, even _____ a visit. Now they are only waiting _____
(15)   (16)   (17)

their next vacation to go back.

E. Expressions

Rewrite the following sentences, replacing the italicized words with the correct form of the appropriate word or expression.

to cripple	coincidence	congested
to picture	vastness	suffocating
barren	to have the upper hand	automated
	all kidding aside	

1. A severe tractor accident last spring *disabled* the young farm boy.

2. In South Dakota there are many areas where formerly *desolate* land is now fertile and productive.

3. Nowadays, banking in the United States is often *done by machine,* so you can deposit or withdraw money without ever seeing another human being!

4. During the month of December, the department stores in Omaha, Nebraska, are *crowded* with shoppers buying presents for the holidays.

5. Never having seen the ocean before her cruise, the girl from Kansas was amazed by its *immensity.*

6. In the early 1870s, Wichita, Kansas was the cowboy capital of the country, but by 1880 the farmers *were in control,* and the cowboys moved on to Dodge City.

7. Historic Front Street in Dodge City, Kansas makes it easy for tourists *to imagine* the rough cowboy town of the 1880s.

8. The moist, *heavy* heat made Lisa wish that her car had air conditioning.

9. *Seriously,* Steve, the northeast corner of Iowa really is called the "Little Switzerland of Iowa" because of its beautiful hills and forests.

10. When Lisa chose a boarding house, she was totally unaware that the owner had known her grandparents—it was just an *accidental occurrence.*

F. Express Yourself

1. What industries or public services have become partially or fully *automated* in the past decade? Which ones do you think will be next? How do you feel about *automation,* and what are its pros and cons?

2. If you have a cold and go to see a doctor, you may be asked if you're *congested*. What do you think this means?

3. In your family, who has *the upper hand*? Your mother? Your father? You? Your spouse? What do you think these other expressions with *hand* mean?
   a. The decision was *in the hands of* the chairman.
   b. The situation got *out of hand*.
   c. She now has the situation *in hand*.
   d. The man was taken to court for his *underhanded* business deals.

G. Think Back

Answer the following questions according to the text.

1. Why did Lisa's grandparents move east?

2. What is the nickname of the Great Plains and why?

3. What good point did Lisa make about people and their surroundings?

4. In what way did Mr. Baker support his statement that nature had the upper hand on the Great Plains?

5. Why is Arbor Day an important holiday on the prairie?

H. Talk About It

1. Does your family still live where your grandparents lived? If not, what were the reasons for any moves?

2. Did your grandparents tell you special stories when you were a child? What were they about?

3. Do you believe that man can control nature? In what ways, yes? In what ways, no?

4. Does your native country have any national holidays related to an aspect of nature similar to Arbor Day in the United States? Explain.

I. Words, Words, Words!

The following vocabulary items have been taken from Lisa's article. Try to guess the meaning of each word from the context and write your definition in the space provided. When you have finished, check the vocabulary list at the end of the book for the correct meaning.

1. ambivalent _____
   The exciting opportunity to travel across the United States also meant leaving family and friends for a few months, so Lisa was somewhat *ambivalent* about her assignment.

2. arid _____
   The fertile, green fields of Iowa contrast sharply with the *arid* plains of the Dakotas.

3. degenerate _____
   Dusty country roads *degenerate* into muddy lanes during the spring rains.

4. deplorable _____
   The roof had holes in it and the windows were broken; in short, the old farmhouse which had stood empty for years was in *deplorable* condition.

5. despair _____
   Throughout their lives, people experience many emotional ups and downs ranging from *despair* to great joy.

6. disarm _____
   After carefully *disarming* the cattle thieves, the police locked the guns in the police car.

7. doomed _____
   Without the life-giving rain the wheat crop was *doomed.*

8. foster _____
   Farm life *fosters* close relationships among family members because of its need for team work.

9. harsh _____
   Harsh winters in Minnesota mean many feet of snow and subzero temperatures.

10. hostile _____
    Early settlers on the Great Plains had to protect themselves from *hostile* animals.

11. initially _____
    Initially, Wall Drugstore in Wall, South Dakota was a small pharmacy. Now the famous store covers a city block.

12. plight _____
    In his book, *Giants in the Earth,* Ole Rölvaag described the *plight* of Scandinavian settlers as they struggled to stay alive during the cold Dakota winters.

13. portray _____
    Meredith Wilson *portrayed* life in a small Iowa town in his musical, "The Music Man."

14. propel _____
    The small motor *propelled* the fishing boat quietly up the Missouri River.

15. self-esteem _____
    The child's *self-esteem* increased when the teacher complimented him on his work.

Wounded Knee, South Dakota, 1973. Waiting for change.

J. Headline

THE PLIGHT OF THE NATIVE AMERICAN
by Lisa Evans

1   December 1890, Wounded Knee, South Dakota. On a cold winter day the small village of Wounded Knee became the scene of the last Indian massacre[1] in the United States. While the United States Cavalry[2] was disarming a group of Sioux Indians, a gun went off. The nervous cavalrymen immediately panicked and opened fire, killing most of the 350 unarmed Indians. Few were able to escape into the frozen prairie.

2   February 27, 1973, Wounded Knee, South Dakota. Less than one hundred years later, Wounded Knee almost witnessed a second Indian disaster. In protest against intolerable living conditions, a group of several hundred armed Indians took over the small village. As a shocked nation watched, the FBI and local police, armed with machine guns, surrounded the Indian protesters. Finally, after 70 days, the Indians sur-

rendered, but not until they had focused national attention on the critical issue of Indian rights.

3   Indian rights have generally been ignored since European settlers established the first settlement in New England at Plymouth, Massachusetts in 1620. The Native Americans who had initially greeted the Pilgrims with gifts of food, soon found themselves in direct conflict with the newcomers over land. Early attempts at goodwill on both sides were replaced by ambivalent feelings which later degenerated into mistrust and fear. In a movement which lasted more than two centuries, the white men pushed westward, their increasing need and desire for land propelling them deeper and deeper into new Indian territory. They justified this movement through the notion of "Manifest Destiny," the belief that white settlers were destined to populate the continent from coast to coast.

4   The Indians fought against the white men, but they were doomed to defeat. Unable to compete with the large armies and guns of the colonists, the various tribes[3] were gradually driven from their lands.

5   Throughout the eighteenth and nineteenth centuries the United States government made treaties with the Indians, agreements in which the government promised to pay cash or merchandise for huge areas of land; however, these promises were repeatedly broken. The Indians fought battle after battle and signed treaty after treaty until they finally had no more land to lose.

6   As early as 1786, the United States government began to establish reservations, large areas of land where the Indians could live apart from the white settlers. But as the white man's desire for land continued to grow, the reservations became smaller and smaller. Furthermore, in most cases, the land "reserved" for the Indians was poor, arid land that the settlers did not want. To-

day, although Indians may choose where they want to live, the majority remain on the reservations. Lacking education and marketable skills, they are poorly equipped to begin a new life in the city.

7   History books and Hollywood westerns have created stereotypes of both the Indians and their white counterparts. Traditionally, Indians have been portrayed as ignorant, murdering savages; the whites, on the other hand, have been described as brave adventurers, struggling to make homes in a new and hostile land. It is not surprising that over the years the Indians have developed a sense of personal and cultural inferiority and the whites a sense of superiority. These feelings are particularly evident on the reservations. Government reservations have fostered a "paternalistic" attitude of whites toward Indians, that is, Indians have been encouraged to be dependent upon whites for food and survival. It should come as no surprise that Indians, after years of isolation and dependency on reservations, often lack motivation and self-esteem.

8   In an attempt to escape from a life of poverty and unemployment, many Indians turn to alcohol. Alcoholism is a major health problem on reservations and in some way affects approximately 80 percent of the families. As one Sioux Indian explained, "When you've got no job, no money, and a house with a dirt roof, you've got good reason to want to get drunk."[4]

9   Despair has even harsher consequences. The suicide rate among Indian teenagers is four times the national average. Traditionally, Indian schools have tried to force children to forget their Indian language and culture in favor of white customs and values. As a result, many young people feel inferior to the average white American and are ashamed of their Indian heritage. Recently, however, this deplorable situation has begun to change through the efforts of sensitive teachers and school administrators.

10   The recent confrontation at Wounded Knee was a painful reminder of the countless crimes committed against the Indians throughout the history of the United States. A new awareness and appreciation of Indian culture has been developing ever since. After more than two centuries of suffering, the Native American is finally on the road to social and economic equality.

Notes

1. massacre: the killing of a large number of people.
2. cavalry: a section of the army in which the soldiers ride on horseback.
3. tribe: a group of Indian families who live and work together.
4. Robert Burnette and John Foster, *The Road to Wounded Knee* (New York: Bantam Books, Inc., 1974).

K. First Impressions

Do the following exercise without referring to the article. Circle the letter next to the statement that best answers the question.

1. According to the article, what was the main reason for the Indian protest at Wounded Knee in 1973?
   a. Indians were forced to live on the reservation.
   b. The Indians wanted more land.
   c. Living conditions on the reservation were unbearable.
   d. There was no reason. They just wanted to cause trouble.

2. Initially, the Indians and early white settlers
   a. got along well with each other.
   b. mistrusted each other.
   c. fought over land.
   d. ignored each other.

3. Throughout the past two centuries, reservations have generally encouraged Indians to
   a. be dependent upon whites for their needs.
   b. feel proud of their Indian heritage.
   c. become a part of the surrounding white culture.
   d. be motivated in their work.

4. A "treaty" is a(n)
   a. piece of land.
   b. agreement.
   c. gift.
   d. amount of money or merchandise.

5. Which of the following is true?
    a. All Indian children feel ashamed of their native heritage.
    b. Government regulations require Indian school children to give up their native language.
    c. There is a high suicide rate among Indian teenagers.
    d. Both a and c.
    e. None of the above.

6. According to the article, why do most Indians remain on reservations?
    a. They do not speak English.
    b. Government regulations force them to live on reservations.
    c. They lack the education and skills that are important for life in the city.
    d. Life on the reservation is so pleasant that no one wishes to leave.

L. Rapid Reading

Do this exercise in class. Scan the article quickly to find the following pieces of information. Write down the number of the paragraph in which each topic is discussed.

a. _____ the establishment of government reservations

b. _____ Manifest Destiny

c. _____ stereotypes

d. _____ a high suicide rate

e. _____ treaties

M. Between the Lines

Circle the letter next to the statement that best answers the question. You may refer to the text.

1. The main idea of the article is
    a. the high rate of suicide and alcoholism among Native Americans.
    b. reservations in the United States.
    c. the history of Indian oppression.
    d. Indian protests in American history.

2. In paragraph 1, the article states that the cavalrymen opened fire. In this context, "opened fire" means
   a. set up camp for the night.
   b. started a large fire.
   c. became angry.
   d. started shooting.

3. In paragraph 4, sentence 2, "their" refers to
   a. the tribes.
   b. the army.
   c. the white colonists.
   d. the Pilgrims.

4. The phrase "ever since" in paragraph 10, sentence 2, refers to the time of
   a. the last Indian massacre in the United States.
   b. the arrival of white settlers in Massachusetts.
   c. the protest at Wounded Knee in 1973.
   d. the introduction of bicultural programs into Indian schools.

5. The article states in paragraph 3, sentence 2, that the Indians and white settlers were in direct conflict. In this context, the word, "conflict" is pronounced
   a. con' flict
   b. con flict'

6. The general tone of Lisa's article is
   a. sympathetic.
   b. revolutionary.
   c. impartial.
   d. militant.

N. More Expressions

Fill in the blanks with words from the following list. Use the correct voice, tense, and singular or plural form of the noun.

initially	self-esteem	harsh
to foster	hostile	ambivalent
to propel	plight	despair
	to portray	

1. The _____ of the buffalo has caused concern among many environmentalists who are worried about the animal becoming extinct.

2. In the 1800s, trains _____ by steam.

3. _____ the Great Plains were a part of the "Wild, Wild West"; now the area is a civilized farming and manufacturing region.

4. Movies _____ the romantic life of cowboys.

5. _____ overwhelmed the people whose homes were destroyed by the tornado.

6. Early river traffic up and down the Mississippi _____ the development of small towns along the river's banks.

7. The young girl's _____ rose when her sheep won first place at the county fair.

8. Cattle ranchers were _____ toward sheep ranchers because of competition for grazing land.

9. In Mark Twain's book *Tom Sawyer*, Aunt Polly was often _____ with her fun-loving nephew.

10. Many early settlers were _____ about leaving the security of a town for the unknown of the wilderness.

O. Express Yourself

1. Is *self-esteem* necessary for happiness? How does your opinion of yourself affect your life and your relationships with others?

2. Pretend you are writing a newspaper article entitled "The *Plight* of _____." How would you finish the headline, and what would your article say?

3. What do you think a *foster* parent and a *foster* home are?

P. Talk It Up

1. How did the early white settlers justify their taking Indian land?

2. What is a treaty? What happened to most of the treaties between the Indians and the United States government?

3. The article stated that reservations have fostered a "paternalistic attitude" of whites toward Indians. What does this mean?

4. The battle between Native Americans and the United States government over land has moved to the courts. Several Native American tribes are trying to recover the land they lost when their treaties were broken. Of course, other people are now living on the land and many have made their homes there for generations. Who do you think are the rightful owners of the land? Can you think of any possible solutions to the problem?

Q. Word Families

Choose the appropriate form of the word. Be certain to use the correct verb tense, singular or plural form of the noun, and the passive voice where necessary.

1. (in)tolerance, to tolerate, (in)tolerable, (in)tolerant
   a. People who do not like cold weather find winters on the Great Plains _____.
   b. Southerners, in general, have a low _____ for cold.
   c. They cannot _____ the snow and freezing temperatures of the Midwest.
   d. _____ people will refuse to travel to the Midwest during the winter months.

2. automation, to automate, automated
   a. _____ has made life easier for many farmers.
   b. The planting and harvesting of crops are now completely _____.
   c. Many farmers would like _____ other processes on their farms, but they cannot afford the initial high cost.

3. ambivalence, ambivalent
   a. The rancher was _____ toward the discovery of oil on his land.
   b. The decision of whether to stay in the city or return to the reservation aroused feelings of _____ in the Hopi Indian.

4. prediction, unpredictability, to predict, predictable, unpredictable
   a. Meteorologists try _____ the weather.
   b. However, their _____ are often wrong.
   c. Tornados, for example, are very _____; no one knows exactly which path they will follow.
   d. This _____ makes them especially dangerous.
   e. Scientists are trying to determine the weather conditions that cause tornados; eventually the storms may become more _____.

5. competition, to compete, competitive
   a. _____ feelings created problems for the early settlers and Indians in North America.
   b. The newcomers and Native Americans _____ for the same land.
   c. _____ for land has repeatedly been a source of conflict throughout world history.

6. portrayal, to portray, portrait
   a. Many of Mark Twain's books _____ life along the Mississippi River.
   b. His book, *Adventures of Huckleberry Finn,* is an excellent _____ of a young boy growing up in nineteenth century Missouri.
   c. A _____ of Mark Twain hangs in his boyhood home in Hannibal, Missouri.

7. propeller, to propel
   a. Early airplane _____ were made of wood instead of metal.
   b. A strong interest in law _____ Abraham Lincoln into a career in politics.

8. ignorance, to ignore, ignorant
   a. Until recently, many history books _____ the deplorable treatment of Native Americans by the United States government during the eighteenth and nineteenth centuries.
   b. As a result, many children have been _____ of this part of American history.
   c. This _____ is rapidly disappearing thanks to new texts and well-informed teachers.

9. conflict, to conflict, conflicting
   a. A _____ has always existed between cattle and sheep ranchers on the Great Plains.
   b. The grazing requirements of cattle and sheep _____.
   c. These _____ needs have led to serious quarrels among the ranchers.

10. impression, to impress, impressive
    a. The Mayo Clinic in Rochester, Minnesota makes a big _____ on visitors from all over the world.
    b. People _____ by the high quality of medical care at the clinic.
    c. In addition to a hospital, the clinic also has _____ research facilities.

R. Look It Up

1. What is the origin of the American holiday, Thanksgiving, and how were the Indians involved? What special foods eaten on this day are of Native American origin?

2. Look up the Badlands in an encyclopedia. How does it describe the area?

3. There are over 400 tribes of Native Americans in the United States, including the Cheyenne, Hopi, Cherokee, Sioux, and Navaho tribes, to name just a few. Choose one tribe and find out something about it; for example, where did they live and what were they known for?

4. Find Mount Rushmore on the map. Which presidents are associated with Mount Rushmore and why?

5. Many Indian words have been incorporated into the English language, including the names of many states and rivers. What do the following words mean: Minnesota, Iowa, Mississippi? Look on a map of the United States and see if you can pick out a few names of states, cities, and rivers that are of Indian origin.

6. Who was Samuel Clemens better known as?

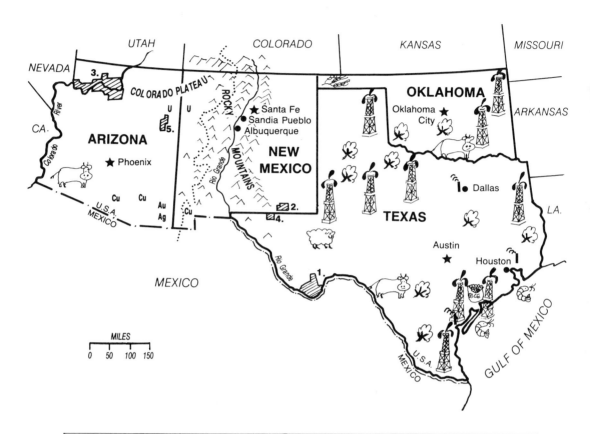

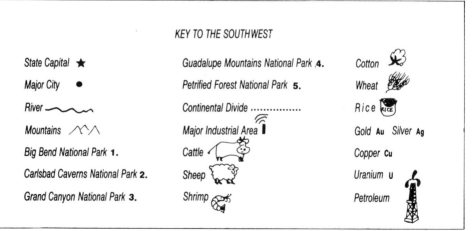

KEY TO THE SOUTHWEST

State Capital ★	Guadalupe Mountains National Park ,**4.**	Cotton	
Major City ●	Petrified Forest National Park **5.**	Wheat	
River ～～	Continental Divide ⋯⋯⋯⋯	Rice	
Mountains ∧∧∧	Major Industrial Area	Gold **Au** Silver **Ag**	
Big Bend National Park **1.**	Cattle	Copper **Cu**	
Carlsbad Caverns National Park **2.**	Sheep	Uranium **U**	
Grand Canyon National Park **3.**	Shrimp	Petroleum	

chapter 7

The Southwest

A. Take a Look

I. Answer the following questions by looking at the map:

1. Which state is the richest in precious metals?

2. Which crop is grown in northwestern Oklahoma?

3. The Rio Grande cuts across which state?

4. What industries do Oklahoma and Texas have in common?

5. Where is the Grand Canyon located?

6. What state capital tells you the name of the state?

II. Make up questions that could be answered by the following information:

1. Sheep

2. In both Arizona and New Mexico

3. New Mexico, Oklahoma, Arkansas, and Louisiana

4. In the southeastern corner of New Mexico

5. Because the Rio Grande makes a big curve at that spot

B. A Letter from Lisa

Sante Fe, New Mexico
July 7

Dear Steve,

I feel like I've been on the road for years instead of days. The trip down to New Mexico from Kansas was hot, dry, and long, even though I made only one detour. Not knowing when I'd be in this part of the country again, I decided to visit Oklahoma City, which wasn't on my route, initially. What a strange place! There are oil derricks[1] absolutely everywhere—on people's lawns, in parks, and even right next to the Governor's mansion! The derricks may have brought prosperity to the state, but if you want my opinion, they stick out like sore thumbs in an otherwise pretty city.

After a day visiting Oklahoma's capital, I headed west again. For a change, I avoided the major highways and stayed on a less-traveled, longer, but much more scenic route. So now I'm finally in New Mexico, a state which certainly merits its nickname, the "Land of Enchantment." I drove into Santa Fe yesterday, and what a welcome change of pace! After driving through the desert for the past few days, this city is like an oasis.[2] There are lots of trees, and the air is cooler; I can even see snow on the tops of the mountains towering over the city. It won't be easy to return to the desert tomorrow, that's for sure!

Santa Fe has a really fascinating history, too. I didn't know it was the second oldest city in the United States, did you? It dates back to 1609 when it was founded by the Spanish. As a matter of fact, it's also the location of the oldest public building in the United States, the Governor's Palace of Santa Fe, which was built a year later in 1610.

But we're still talking about relatively recent history. Long before the Spanish ever thought about establishing a colony here, Santa Fe was already the home of the Pueblo Indians. Just a little south of Santa Fe, there's the tiny Indian pueblo[3] of Sandia. It's amazing to think that it may have been inhabited since 1300. That makes the Governor's Palace seem almost modern in comparison, doesn't it?

Today, when I look around me in Santa Fe, I see the influences of both the Native Americans and the Spanish. According to my guidebook, the two groups successfully intermarried over the centuries, which not only created a new culture, but also encouraged their feelings of mutual respect. In the late 1800s when the "Anglo"[4] settlers began arriving in Santa Fe, apparently they, too, followed this pattern of intercultural cooperation. In fact, as far as I can see, this pattern seems to have become an established tradition here.

This morning I decided to walk through the narrow, winding streets to the Central Plaza and leave my car at the hotel. I like to walk because I get a better sense of the city, and besides, I wanted a closer look at the adobe houses. What a change from basic Boston brick! Yesterday when I was still a short distance from Santa Fe, I had the strange impression that its buildings were a part of the landscape. The sun was setting and there was a beautiful orange glow to everything. When I got into the city, I realized that most of the buildings were made of adobe, an earthen mixture of straw and mud. Since the houses are made of the same mud as the streets, their colors blend together, and it is hard to tell from a distance where the streets end and the walls begin.

I also found out that adobe brick is a real energy saver. It keeps the heat out during the summer and keeps it in during the winter. The Pueblo Indians are the ones who can take the credit for this "modern" solution to the energy crisis. They were already using adobe bricks hundreds of years ago, long before energy conservation was even necessary!

When I finally got to the Central Plaza, I saw dozens of woven blankets spread out on the sidewalks in front of the Governor's Palace. Since 1610, the Indians have been coming to this spot to sell their exquisite jewelry, basketry, pottery, and other handicrafts which they carefully display on the blankets. So apparently, Sante Fe can boast of having not only the oldest public building, but also America's oldest shopping center, as the Central Plaza is often jokingly called. I might add that only the Indians are allowed to sell in front of the Governor's Palace—one good example of Santa Fe's respect for tradition.

Tomorrow I head north, away from Santa Fe, but toward the Grand Canyon on my way to Utah.

Adiós![5]

Lisa

P.S. Did you ever learn Spanish? Well, there's a famous hotel that used to mark the end of the old Santa Fe Trail[6] called the La Fonda Hotel. If I remember my high school Spanish correctly, "la fonda" means "the hotel," so I guess it translates as "the The Hotel hotel"![7]

Notes

1. oil derrick: a tall structure used in drilling for oil.
2. oasis: a fertile spot in a very dry area.
3. pueblo: a communal dwelling that is found in the villages of some southwestern Indians and consists of flat-roofed stone or adobe houses attached in groups sometimes several stories high.
4. Anglo: a term referring to people of English descent.
5. adiós: a common expression in Spanish for good-bye.

6. The Santa Fe Trail: a pioneer route to the Southwest that was used throughout the 19th century. It stretched from Kansas City, Missouri to Santa Fe, New Mexico.
7. Ernie Pyle, *Home Country* (New York: William Sloane Associates, Inc., 1947).

C. True or False?

Write T before those statements that are true and F before those that are false.

_____ 1. Lisa drove straight from Kansas to New Mexico.
_____ 2. Lisa thinks that Oklahoma City would be prettier without the oil derricks.
_____ 3. In general, Lisa takes less-traveled, longer, but much more scenic routes.
_____ 4. Santa Fe is the oldest city in the United States.
_____ 5. The Pueblo Indians got their name from the houses they lived in.
_____ 6. Many of Santa Fe's inhabitants are a mixture of Native American and Spanish descent.
_____ 7. Lisa says that she likes to walk because she needs the exercise.
_____ 8. The color of adobe contrasts beautifully with Santa Fe's landscape.
_____ 9. Adobe homes tend to be hot in the summer and cold in the winter.
_____ 10. Indians have been selling their handicrafts in the Central Plaza for centuries.

D. Close-up

Fill in the blanks with a, an, or the. If no article is necessary, put an X in the blank.

Lisa had never imagined what _____ fascinating city Santa Fe was. To
           (1)

begin with, she learned that it is _____ second oldest city in _____
           (2)   (3)

United States, and was founded by _____ Spanish in _____ beginning
           (4)   (5)

of _____ seventeenth century. In _____ Central Plaza of _____ Santa
   (6)   (7)   (8)

Fe is _____ Governor's Palace, _____ interesting example of _____
    (9)   (10)   (11)

Spanish architecture and also _____ oldest public building in _____
(12)   (13)

country. After taking _____ tour of _____ Governor's Palace, Lisa had
(14)   (15)

_____ lunch near _____ Plaza in _____ little restaurant which
(16)   (17)   (18)

served _____ Mexican food. There, she once again opened up her
(19)

guidebook and began reading more about _____ history of Santa Fe.
(20)

E. Expressions

Rewrite the following sentences, replacing the italicized words with the correct form of the appropriate word or expression.

a change of pace	to merit	otherwise
as far as I can see	to found	mutual
to boast(of)	landscape	to make a detour

to stick out like a sore thumb

1. A flat tire in Amarillo, Texas was the only problem on Lisa's *in all other respects* uneventful trip from Oklahoma to New Mexico.

2. Sometimes campers in the Southwest get tired of roughing it, so for *something different* they rent a motel room for the night and go to a nice restaurant.

3. The Navaho Nation, located mainly in Arizona, can *brag about* being the single largest Indian nation in the United States.

4. Carlsbad Caverns used to be called "Bat Cave" and, *based on what I know*, it still deserves the name because bats continue to fly though the caverns during the summer months.

5. Oklahoma and Texas have many industries *in common*, the best known of which is oil.

6. Port Arthur, Texas has the largest petroleum refinery in the country, and consequently *deserves* its title of "Energy City."

7. The main road between Santa Fe and Taos was closed for construction, forcing Lisa *to take an alternate route*.

8. St. Augustine, Florida, the oldest city in the United States, *was established* in 1565, 44 years before Santa Fe.

9. Organ Pipe Cactus National Monument on Arizona's Mexican border was so named because its *scenery* includes cacti whose thirty or more "arms" resemble organ pipes.

10. The enormous billboard *looked ugly* in the middle of the beautiful field in New Mexico.

F. Express Yourself

1. Where do you think the expression *"stick out like a sore thumb"* comes from?

2. For a *change of pace* from the busy newspaper office, Steve relaxes at his house by the seashore. What do you like to do for a *change of pace*?

3. Think of your best friend or your spouse. What are some of your *mutual* interests?

G. Think Back

Answer the following questions according to the text.

1. Why did Lisa think that Oklahoma City was a strange place?

2. What made Santa Fe a welcome change of pace?

3. What are the three main cultural groups in the Santa Fe region?

4. Why did Lisa have the impression that the buildings were a part of the landscape when she first approached Santa Fe?

5. Name two things that Lisa saw in the Central Plaza.

H. Talk About It

1. What are some handicrafts that are representative of your native country?

2. Many people in the United States are of mixed descent. What is your family's cultural background?

3. What is the oldest city in your native country? When was it founded and by whom?

I. Words, Words, Words!

The following vocabulary items have been taken from Lisa's article. Try to guess the meaning of each word from the context and write your definition in the space provided. When you have finished, check the vocabulary list at the end of the book for the correct meaning.

1. abundance _____
   Fishing is a major industry along the coast of Texas where there is an *abundance* of shrimp.

2. compromise _____
   Steve's friend wanted to live in Mexico, but his wife wanted to stay in the States, so they made a *compromise* and moved to New Mexico.

3. dwindle _____
   The world's population of whooping cranes has *dwindled* over the past years. Now there are only around 80 birds remaining.

4. evaporate _____
   Any rain that falls in the desert *evaporates* quickly in the dry heat.

5. face _____
   Aransas National Wildlife Refuge on the coast of Texas provides a safe winter home for the whooping crane, a bird that is *facing* extinction.

6. mighty _____
   The *mighty* winds of the hurricane caused extensive damage along the Gulf Coast.

7. run out of _____
   When the family on the frontier *ran out of* sugar and salt, they had to ride over 50 miles to replenish their supply.

8. sacrifice _____
   Early settlers had to *sacrifice* many comforts when they left their homes in the East to start a new life on the western frontier.

9. shortage _____
   During the Dust Bowl years in Oklahoma, there was a severe *shortage* of water.

10. survive _____
    Only plants that have adapted to an arid environment can *survive* in the desert.

11. take for granted _____
    Residents of the Southwest often *take* the beauty of their region *for granted*; it takes a tourist like Lisa to appreciate it fully.

The unique beauty of the southwestern desert.

J. Headline

RUNNING DRY?

by Lisa Evans

1   Cracks up to 25 feet wide have formed in the desert between Tucson and Phoenix, Arizona due to a sharp drop in underground water level. Farmland around Pecos, Texas, which was once green and fertile, is now brown and abandoned. Is the Southwest running out of water? People are getting worried.

2   For the past several decades people in the United States have taken water for granted. On the average, each person uses 87 gallons of water a day; of that amount, only two gallons are actually used for cooking and drinking. Flushing the toilet once uses six to eight gallons and taking a five-minute shower can send 25 to 30 gallons down the drain. That's a lot of water! The amount of water consumed indirectly through food and industrial products is also staggering. From start to finish, the egg you had for breakfast required 120 gallons of water; the steak at dinner, 3,500 gallons; the ton of steel in your car, 60,000 gallons.

3   The United States is presently facing serious water problems. Rain and snow do not fall evenly across the country. The Northwest receives an abundance of rain, more than 80 inches each year in some areas. In

contrast, parts of the West and Southwest receive less than ten inches per year. The Northeast and Midwest traditionally have had sufficient supplies of water, but recently both regions have begun to experience water shortages. At one point, while New Yorkers were worrying about having enough water in which to bathe, farmers in Iowa prayed that their crops would survive the hot summer months.

4   One area that has been hit especially hard by the increasing shortage of water is the Southwest. Cacti[1] flourish across its deserts, but crops cannot grow in the dry, sandy soil unless there is extensive irrigation.[2] In some areas, farmland is returning to desert because the life-giving water has run out or become too expensive to pump from deep underground.

5   The Southwest receives its water from primarily two sources: large, underground reserves of water, called acquifers, and the 1,400-mile-long Colorado River. The acquifers, which were formed over thousands of years ago, are being consumed slowly but surely. More water is taken out than nature can replace. The acquifers receive only 8 percent of the total precipitation;[3] the remaining 92 percent either evaporates or flows unused into the ocean.

6   The Ogallala Acquifer[4] stretches 800 miles from western Texas to northern Nebraska. This underground reserve of fresh water, containing enough water to fill Lake Huron, is perhaps the largest in the world. Nevertheless, its water level is steadily dropping. If water consumption continues at the present rate, the Ogallala may be dry in 40 more years. A conservationist in Texas compares the problem to "taking money out of a checking account faster than you put it in; sooner or later you're going to come up with a zero balance."[5]

7   The beautiful Colorado River has caused nearly as many fights in the West and Southwest as gold or whiskey ever did. This precious source of water flows through Wyoming, Utah, Nevada, Colorado, Arizona, New Mexico, California, and Mexico. Each of the seven states as well as Mexico has a legal right to a portion of its water; however, for years, California has been using not only its share of water but also a part of Arizona's to supply water for Los Angeles and the surrounding area. People from Arizona and the mountain states resent this and feel their water is being stolen. By the time the river actually reaches its goal, the Gulf of California, there is no longer much water left to fight over. After Mexico claims its 10 percent share for irrigation, the once mighty Colorado becomes a trickle and gradually disappears into the sand.

8   Now that the days of cheap and plentiful water are over, it is clear that sacrifices have to be made. The question is, who will make them? The farmers feel that as they supply a high percentage of the nation's food, they need the water to keep their farms alive and the country well-fed. Oil and coal companies, on the other hand, feel their need for water is greater because they provide the country with important sources of energy. In addition, the demand for water for personal use is growing as more and more people are moving to the sunny, warm climate of the Southwest. Retirement communities, such as Sun City, Arizona, which form green oases in the desert, are becoming increasingly popular. And the population of Los Angeles shows no sign of decreasing.

9   So, while resources are dwindling, needs are growing. It is clearly time for both conservation and compromise in the use of our most valuable resource, water.

Notes

1. cactus (plural: cactuses, cacti): a desert plant with sharp thorns instead of leaves.
2. irrigation: the process of providing water for land and crops.
3. precipitation: the water that falls to the earth.
4. The acquifer is named after the Ogallala Indians of the Great Plains.
5. balance: the amount of money in a bank account. From *Newsweek* 23 February 1981: p. 30.

K. First Impressions

Do the following exercise without referring to the article. Circle the letter next to the statement(s) that best answer(s) the question.

1. According to the article, the major problem of the Southwest is
   a. irrigation.
   b. a shortage of water.
   c. too much precipitation.
   d. the energy crisis.

2. What are the *two* main sources of water for the Southwest?
   a. Acquifers.
   b. Water from snow and rain.
   c. The Colorado River.
   d. The Gulf of California.

3. The area of the United States that receives the most precipitation is
   a. the Northwest.
   b. the Northeast.
   c. the Southwest.
   d. the Midwest.

4. Which of the following statements about the Colorado River is false?
   a. It flows through two countries.
   b. It has been the cause of many fights in the Southwest.
   c. Its water is divided equally among seven states.
   d. The mouth of the river is on the Gulf of California.

5. The United States is presently experiencing a water shortage because
   a. people take water for granted.
   b. no precipitation falls in the Southwest.
   c. the need for water is increasing.
   d. both a and c.
   e. both b and c.

L. Rapid Reading

Do this exercise in class. Scan the article quickly to find the following pieces of information. Write down the number of the paragraph in which each topic is discussed.

a. _____ the size of the Ogallala Acquifer

b. _____ the groups of people competing for water in the Southwest

c. _____ the precipitation across the United States

d. _____ the amount of water consumed daily by each individual

e. _____ the partition of the Colorado River

M. Between the Lines

Circle the letter next to the statement that best answers the question. You may refer to the text.

1. The main idea of the article is that
   a. people shouldn't take long showers.
   b. we need to find new sources of water.
   c. we need to conserve our water supplies.
   d. the Ogallala Acquifer is running dry.

2. In paragraph 2, the article states that the amount of water consumed indirectly is staggering. What does the word "staggering" mean in this context?
   a. Faint from lack of water.
   b. Surprising.
   c. Walking unsteadily.

3. In paragraph 3, the article states that precipitation does not fall evenly across the United States. What does the word "evenly" mean in this context?
   a. Exactly.
   b. Horizontally.
   c. Equally.

4. In paragraph 6, sentence 3, "its water level" refers to the water level of
   a. the Colorado River.
   b. Lake Huron.
   c. the Ogallala Acquifer.
   d. the Gulf of California.

5. To say that the Colorado River has caused nearly as many fights as gold or whiskey ever did implies that
   a. the water of the Colorado is extremely valuable.
   b. it costs a lot to get a drink of water on the Colorado River.
   c. historically, there have been many fights near the river.

6. In paragraph 7, the article states that the Colorado River has become a trickle. In this context, the word "trickle" means
   a. to flow slowly.
   b. a thin stream.
   c. a drop of water.
7. What is the main idea of paragraph 8?
   a. The farmers need the most water to supply the nation with food.
   b. Sacrifices will have to be made among the different groups in the Southwest.
   c. Oil and coal companies need water to solve the nation's energy crisis.

N. More Expressions

Fill in the blanks with words from the following list. Use the correct voice, tense, and singular or plural form of the noun.

to take for granted	to dwindle	shortage
to run out of	abundance	to sacrifice
compromise	to face	to survive
	mighty	

1. When the oil refinery went bankrupt, its workers _____ probable unemployment.

2. The group of hikers _____ time while they were walking down into the Grand Canyon, so they had to turn around and come back.

3. Arizona has a(n) _____ of copper and produces 50 percent of the nation's supply.

4. The _____ forces of nature shaped the land in Monument Valley on the Arizona–Utah border into strange but magnificent formations.

5. Lisa _____ her day off so that she could finish her article.

6. There is no _____ of wool in New Mexico, where sheep raising is a major industry.

7. The Civil War was the result of the northern and southern states' inability to reach a _____.

8. So far, in many Indian villages, century-old traditions _____ the pressures from modern civilization.

9. Interest in building another dam on the Colorado River _____ after environmentalist groups protested strongly.

10. Travelers in the desert quickly learn not _____ water
_____.

O. Express Yourself

1. What are some aspects of your everyday life that you had *taken for granted* before you left home?
2. If you were describing your native country to someone, what would you say it had an *abundance* of?
3. Is it possible to *run out of* patience? If so, when was the last time you *ran out of* patience and why?

P. Talk It Up

1. How has the water shortage affected the landscape of the Southwest?
2. What is an acquifer?
3. Why is the water level of the Ogallala dropping?
4. In paragraph 2 of the article, it says that 3,500 gallons of water were required to produce a steak. How is this possible?
5. Think of all the ways you waste water. What could you do to conserve it?
6. Role play. Roles: Farmer(s), Miner(s), Mayor (City Council) of Los Angeles, concerned citizen(s) from Arizona, advisory board members of the Colorado River Water Commission. Prepare and then present your argument for why you should receive the largest share of water. The advisory board members will ask questions and then come to a decision based upon what they have heard.

Q. Word Families

Choose the appropriate form of the word. Be certain to use the correct verb tense, singular or plural form of the noun, and the passive voice where necessary.

1. resentment, to resent, resentful, resentfully
   a. Farmers in Arizona are _____ of their Californian neighbors, who use more than their share of water from the Colorado River.
   b. The Indians of the Southwest, who had their own religion, _____ the early attempts of the Spanish missionaries to convert them to Christianity.
   c. Commercial fishermen along the Texas coast felt considerable _____ toward the company that was responsible for the oil spill.
   d. They _____ complained to both the state and federal governments about its effect upon fishing.

2. survivor, survival, to survive, surviving
   a. A person can _____ for only a few days without water before dying of dehydration.

b. The _____ of the mountain climbing expedition in the New Mexican Rockies were taken by ambulance to the hospital.

c. The newspaper listed the _____ relatives of the deceased climbers.

d. The _____ of the farming industry in the Southwest will depend upon the future condition of the acquifers.

3. decision, to decide, decisive, decisively

   a. In 1830 the United States government _____ to make Oklahoma an Indian Territory.

   b. This _____ led to the establishment of a large Indian settlement in the state.

   c. Lisa acted _____ and bought the Navaho Indian rug that she had been admiring in the shop.

   d. His eight successful years of experience in Congress gave the Democratic senator from Oklahoma a _____ advantage over his inexperienced Republican opponent.

4. fascination, to fascinate, fascinating, fascinated

   a. The beauty of Carlsbad Caverns _____ tourists for decades.

   b. No one knows for sure how far the _____ network of caverns extends into the Guadalupe Mountains.

   c. _____ visitors are guided through underground rooms filled with magnificent limestone sculptures.

   d. The girl's _____ with caves led her to become a geologist.

5. basis, to base, basic, basically

   a. Lisa feels that although Boston has its faults, it is _____ a nice place to live.

   b. Most of the colorful Indian dances have a religious_____.

   c. The Hopi Snake Dance _____ upon the belief that the snakes will tell the gods of the Indians' need for rain.

   d. Lisa's guidebook gave her a _____ knowledge of Santa Fe's history.

6. imagination, to imagine, imaginary, imaginative

   a. The Wild West comes alive in Tombstone, Arizona for the person who uses his _____.

   b. One can easily _____ rough cowboys and gunmen walking through the town's dusty streets.

   c. An _____ architect designed the ultramodern building for the art museum in Houston.

   d. The snakes carried by Indians in the Hopi Snake Dance are real, not _____.

7. relationship, relative, to relate, relatively

   a. The hotel in Santa Fe was _____ inexpensive compared to the one where Lisa stayed in Cape Canaveral.

b. The professor at the University of Oklahoma has a good _____ with her students because she _____ well to young people.

c. Those interested in early American art and furniture will want to visit the Houston home of the late Miss Ima Hogg, a _____ of James S. Hogg, the first native-born governor of Texas.

8. necessity, to necessitate, necessary, necessarily
   a. The increasing demand for water in the Southwest has made water conservation _____.
   b. Heavy snow _____ closing roads on the north rim of the Grand Canyon in winter.
   c. Taking photographs is not _____ allowed on Indian reservations, so it is a good idea to ask first.
   d. The _____ of finding new oil reserves has led to more drilling in the Gulf of Mexico.

9. comparison, to compare, comparable, comparatively
   a. When shopping it is important _____ the prices and quality of goods.
   b. Although the prices of the two rugs in the shop were _____, the quality of the Navaho rug was much better.
   c. After traveling across the Great Plains, Lisa felt that the drive to Utah would seem _____ short.
   d. The state of Texas is huge in _____ to Rhode Island.

10. to harden, hard, hardly
    a. Lisa worked _____ on her article for several hours before going out to dinner.
    b. It was _____ for her to leave Santa Fe.
    c. The homemade ice cream _____ after it had been in the freezer for an hour.
    d. It _____ ever rains in Phoenix; the city has more than 200 perfectly clear days every year.

R. Look It Up

1. What is a "cowlick," and where did the expression come from?

2. How was Carlsbad Caverns discovered? What are stalagmites and stalactites?

3. Find a list of state nicknames. Pick two and try to guess their origins.

4. How did the city of Phoenix get its name?

5. The Santa Fe Trail played an important part in the development of the West. Look up some information on the trail and the people who used it.

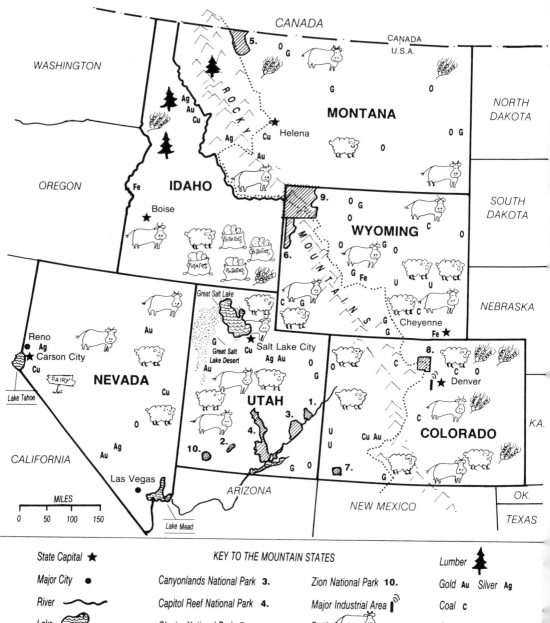

CANADA

CANADA
U.S.A.

WASHINGTON

OREGON

CALIFORNIA

MONTANA

Helena ★

IDAHO

Boise ★

NEVADA

Reno ●
Carson City ★

Lake Tahoe

Las Vegas ●

MILES
0   50   100   150

Lake Mead

ARIZONA

Great Salt Lake

Salt Lake City ★

Great Salt
Lake Desert

UTAH

10.   2.   4.   3.   1.

7.

WYOMING

Cheyenne ★

COLORADO

Denver ★

8.

9.

6.

5.

NORTH
DAKOTA

SOUTH
DAKOTA

NEBRASKA

KA.

OK.

TEXAS

NEW MEXICO

OK.

ROCKY   MOUNTAINS

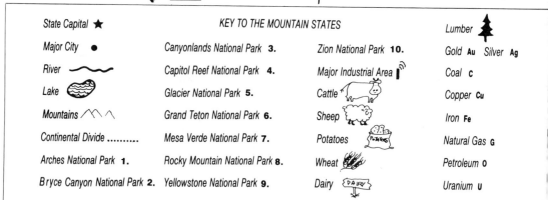

	KEY TO THE MOUNTAIN STATES		
State Capital ★		Zion National Park 10.	Lumber 🌲
Major City ●	Canyonlands National Park 3.	Major Industrial Area	Gold Au Silver Ag
River ～	Capitol Reef National Park 4.	Cattle	Coal c
Lake 🏞	Glacier National Park 5.	Sheep	Copper Cu
Mountains ⋀⋀⋀	Grand Teton National Park 6.	Potatoes	Iron Fe
Continental Divide	Mesa Verde National Park 7.	Wheat	Natural Gas G
Arches National Park 1.	Rocky Mountain National Park 8.	Dairy	Petroleum o
Bryce Canyon National Park 2.	Yellowstone National Park 9.		Uranium U

chapter 8

The Mountain States

A. Take a Look

I. Answer the following questions by looking at the map:

1. In which states are gold, silver, and copper all found?

2. Through which states does the Continental Divide pass?

3. Which state and its capital end in the same letter?

4. Which state has a lake, a desert, and a capital with almost the same name?

5. In which state(s) is wheat grown?

6. Which national parks are located in Utah?

II. Make up questions that could be answered by the following information:

1. Helena

2. Washington and Oregon

3. Potatoes

4. Glacier National Park

5. Northern Idaho and western Montana

B. A Letter from Lisa

Salt Lake City, Utah
July 28

Howdy,[1] Steve!

You get three guesses. Who said, "If there's a place on earth that nobody else wants, that's the place I'm looking for," and then found "the place" near the shores of Great Salt Lake? If you guessed Brigham Young, the Mormon leader, you're right. I'm ashamed to admit that a week ago I wouldn't have known the answer to that question. As soon as I got to Salt Lake City, I did some fast research on the Mormon religion and way of life; otherwise, there's no way I could have fully appreciated a state in which more than 60 percent of the population is Mormon. That would have been like going to Plymouth Rock without knowing who the Pilgrims were!

Actually the Mormons have a very colorful history. I learned that the Mormon Church is a purely American creation, dating back only to 1830 when it was founded in New York state by Joseph Smith, a man who preached that America was God's promised land. As you may remember, though, the Mormons were almost immediately persecuted and forced west because they were polygamists (or rather, the <u>men</u> could have several wives at a time. Talk about unfair!), and polygamy was clearly unacceptable in a monogamous society.

Brigham Young took over when Smith was murdered in Illinois and continued to lead the Mormons west in search of a safe haven. Finally, in July 1847, they reached "the place" in the desert of Utah, where they found land which was constantly plagued by drought, where good soil for cultivating crops was limited, and where the climate was inhospitable; in short, a place nobody else wanted. Just what they were looking for! With true pioneer spirit, Brigham Young and his followers began to plow and irrigate the land. Between 1850 and 1900, the Utah Mormons were joined by more than 90,000 immigrants from all over the world. Out of the desert and wilderness they created what I would consider one of the most beautifully planned cities in the United States.

Salt Lake City seems to have been spared the inner city congestion so common in other metropolitan areas. As it grew, the city retained the Mormon's original spacious layout, designed over 100 years ago, of neat blocks and very wide, tree-lined streets. There are beautiful green parks everywhere and fragrant orchards[2] around every corner. What I couldn't help noticing was how clean the streets and sidewalks were. No litter here!

In the heart of Salt Lake City is the imposing Mormon Temple, the center of Mormonism for more than three million people all over the globe. I wasn't permitted to enter because the Temple's closed to non-Mormons, so I went instead to the nearby Tabernacle[3] to hear the famous Mormon Tabernacle Choir live! Try to imagine being in an enormous room with 375 singing voices accompanied by a massive pipe organ (10,814 pipes to be exact!). It was an unforgettable musical experience, and certainly one of the highlights of this trip.

I don't mean to give you the wrong impression that everything and everyone in Utah is influenced by the Mormon Church. There's nothing particularly "different" about the people here, except maybe that they're especially helpful and friendly. Actually, the only time I felt even slightly awkward was yesterday afternoon when I ordered a glass of wine in a café. I had forgotten that Mormons don't drink, and that in Utah, cocktails[4] and wine can be consumed in public only during a meal at a restaurant, and beer is the only alcoholic beverage served in public bars.

I didn't get out to Great Salt Lake until this afternoon. It's all that's left of a gigantic, prehistoric lake, now a mere twentieth of its original size, but still almost twice as big as the state of Rhode Island! Can you imagine? I'd always heard that it's impossible to sink in this lake, but I never believed it until today. The water is 25 percent salt which makes it <u>ten</u> times saltier than the ocean, so you can literally lie back and relax on top of the water. I had spent about fifteen minutes in that position and was thoroughly enjoying myself when someone swam by and splashed water in my eyes. Ouch! Actually, I needed a good excuse to get out and dry off. The salt was making me really thirsty and I was starting to look like a prune![5]

You know, it's hard for me to imagine that Utah was <u>ever</u> "a place nobody wanted." It's a magnificent state of mountains, lakes, and forests, and has more national parks than any other state except California. Utah is also full of amazing rock formations carved by nature, little by little, over time. On my trip here from Santa Fe, I stopped to watch the sunset in Bryce Canyon National Park. What looked like hundreds of stone fairy castles slowly changed colors with the fading sun—first orange, then pink, deep red, and finally purple. What a spectacle!

Tomorrow, I'm making a small detour to the eastern part of the state. It would be a shame to miss Dinosaur National Monument, the largest collection of prehistoric vertebrates in the United States, when I'm so close. Then it's westward again to Oregon.

Love,

Lisa

P.S. By the way, Steve, in case you were thinking of moving to Utah, polygamy is no longer allowed. As a matter of fact, the Mormon Church now excommunicates those who practice it!

Notes

1. howdy: a colloquial form of "hello," often associated with western cowboys.

2. orchard: a large group of fruit trees.
3. tabernacle: a large building used for religious services.
4. cocktail: a drink in which liquor is mixed with another ingredient.
5. prune: a dried plum.

C. True or False?

Write T before those statements that are true and F before those that are false.

_____ 1. More than half the people in Utah are Mormons.
_____ 2. The Mormon religion was founded by Brigham Young.
_____ 3. Great Salt Lake was once twenty times larger than its present size.
_____ 4. Polygamy is still an accepted part of the Mormon religion.
_____ 5. Lisa was extremely embarrassed when, forgetting Utah's liquor laws, she ordered wine in a café.
_____ 6. After having visited Great Salt Lake, Lisa understood why no one wanted Utah.
_____ 7. Utah has more national parks than any other state in the country.
_____ 8. The Mormon Tabernacle is not open to nonMormons.
_____ 9. The Mormons wanted the land around Great Salt Lake because no one else wanted it.
_____ 10. The Mormon religion is recent, dating back only to the 19th century.

D. Close-up

Fill in the blanks with the appropriate prepositions.

_____ a bad storm _____ Wyoming, a sheepherder named Earl Holding
(1)   (2)

was stranded _____ the towns _____ Rock Springs and Green River.
(3)   (4)

He swore _____ the time that if he survived, he would return _____
(5)   (6)

the same spot and build a haven _____ travelers _____ the area—and
(7)   (8)

he kept his promise. Today, Earl Holding, Jr., now a multimillionaire, is the

manager _____(9) the two reststops, called "Holding's Little Americas,"

which his father built. Both _____(10) them are tourist and trucker stops,

complete _____(11) restaurants, hotels, and most important _____(12) all, gas

stations, each famous _____(13) having the largest number _____(14) gas

pumps _____(15) the world. The two reststops are located approximately a

tank _____(16) gas apart _____(17) the main interstate _____(18) southern

Wyoming. Until recently, there were no other gas stations _____(19) the two

Little Americas, just plenty _____(20) oil wells where, _____(21) course, filling

up was impossible.

E. Expressions

Rewrite the following sentences, replacing the italicized words with the correct form of the appropriate word or expression.

to persecute	fragrant	to spare
haven	to carve	imposing
to retain	literally	to plague
	highlight	

1. There are so many horses in Wyoming that they *actually* outnumber the people living there!

2. In 1848 a flock of seagulls flew into Salt Lake City and ate the crickets that *infested* the crops of the first Mormon farmers, thus earning the nickname of the "Mormon Air Force."

3. Park City, Utah, a former silvermining town, *was saved from* gradual abandonment when a ski resort, which now claims to have the best snow in the country, was established there.

4. Needless to say, for gamblers, Las Vegas is one of the *special stops* of a trip through the West.

5. Idaho *has kept* its reputation as the potato capital of the United States even though the state of Maine claims that its potatoes are superior.

6. The Great Divide Basin in Wyoming is a *place of safety* for the largest herd of wild horses in the United States.

7. Visitors to Yellowstone National Park can see at close range many species of animals including the *impressively large* buffalo, a stocky beast with menacing horns.

8. Sagebrush, the state flower of Nevada, is an *aromatic* plant whose odor resembles that of sage, an herb often used in cooking.

9. After years of *being persistently harassed,* the Indians won temporary relief in 1876 when a group of Sioux killed General Custer and his entire command on the Little Bighorn River in Montana.

10. The mountain goats in Glacier National Park are oblivious to the dangers of falling and move with total self-assurance along the narrow trails they *have precisely cut* in the mountain faces.

F. Express Yourself

1. Which of the following would be *carved,* and who or what would do the *carving?*

   a. initials in a tree
   b. a sand castle
   c. a turkey
   d. an Indian totem pole
   e. a chair
   f. a river
   g. a canyon
   h. roast beef

2. In your own words, what is the difference between discrimination and *persecution?* What groups have been *persecuted* in history?

3. "*Spare*" is used both as a verb and as a noun in many different contexts. Look at the following sentences and figure out what "*spare*" means in each. Which sentences have related meanings?
   a. Lisa had a *spare* tire in the trunk of her car.
   b. Steve was extremely busy and had very little *spare* time.
   c. Parents who are not very strict "*spare* the rod and spoil the child."
   d. Lisa had a very small traveling budget, so she had no money to *spare*.
   e. Lisa stayed with her sister in New York City and so was *spared* the expense of staying in a hotel.

G. Think Back

Answer the following questions according to the text.

1. Who said "This is the place," and to what was he referring?

2. Why were the Mormons persecuted?

3. Describe Salt Lake City. What two buildings would you find in its center?

4. What is the origin of Great Salt Lake and why is it special?

5. Which national park did Lisa visit in Utah and what did the scenery remind her of?

H. Talk About It

1. Lisa maintains that Salt Lake City has been spared the inner city congestion so common in other metropolitan areas. What does she mean, and what contributes to this congestion?

2. Can you think of any countries where polygamy is still practiced at present? Can polygamy be justified, and if so, how?

3. The United States is a country whose government is not affiliated with any particular religion. Many countries do have a religious affiliation, though. Is religion a major influence on your native country's politics? If so, how? If not, what are some countries where religion is very important and how is it influential?

I. Words, Words, Words!

The following vocabulary items have been taken from Lisa's article. Try to guess the meaning of each word from the context and write your definition in the space provided. When you have finished, check the vocabulary list at the end of the book for the correct meaning.

1. accessible _____
   The icy, blue lake in the Grand Tetons was *accessible* by only two trails in the summer.

2. awesome _____
   Visitors of all religions are impressed by the *awesome* Mormon Temple and Tabernacle.

3. bear in mind _____
   When driving through the Rockies in winter, it is good to *bear in mind* that many roads may be closed because of snow.

4. dilemma _____
   Wanting to increase their annual income, states are faced with the *dilemma* of whether or not to legalize the lucrative but often corrupt business of gambling.

5. dwelling _____
   Many Indians lived in *dwellings* called tepees, which were conical shelters made out of animal skins.

6. ensure _____
   Lisa left her motel room early in the morning to *ensure* her arrival at Bryce National Park before sunset.

7. flock _____
   People *flock* to Colorado ski resorts during Christmas vacation, making the slopes crowded.

8. follow suit _____
   First one carload of tourists stopped to watch the bears and then others *followed suit.* Soon the road was impassable.

9. outstanding _____
   The world famous pianist gave an *outstanding* performance in Denver's attractive civic center to the delight of her audience.

10. peer _____
    The cowboy *peered* through the dusty window of the saloon trying to see if his friend was at the bar.

11. unintentionally _____
    Lisa *unintentionally* left her camera in the car when she stopped at the Grand Canyon, so she had to go back for it.

Old Faithful just "letting off steam."

J. Headline

THE NATIONAL PARKS: WHAT TO DO?

by Lisa Evans

1   The edge of the circle is crowded with people. Some of them are sitting on benches; others are standing and shifting impatiently from one foot to the other. A child is pulling on her mother's sleeve and asking for the tenth time, "How much longer, Mommy?" Everyone is waiting. Suddenly, Old Faithful, the star of Yellowstone National Park, makes its grand entrance by shooting a column of boiling water 130 feet into the air. In the next five minutes between 10,000 and 13,000 gallons of water and steam at a temperature of about 205°F. escape from the earth. Fifteen

---

minutes later as the last wisps of steam evaporate high in the air, the benches are empty; the spectators have moved on to other Yellowstone attractions. For Old Faithful there is little time to rest between shows. True to its name, the geyser will faithfully repeat its incredible performance every hour, and already the crowds are beginning to gather for the next show.

2 Every summer more than 30,000 people a day flock to Yellowstone, but even during the colder months the park is open and attracts those visitors who feel that winter is the only time to experience its beauty. The overwhelming crowds have left and the 3,472 square miles of park are quiet and snow-covered. Cross-country skiers can follow trails past magnificent ice sculptures formed by geysers and waterfalls frozen in motion.

3 The idea of preserving areas of outstanding natural beauty through a national park system originated in the United States. Yellowstone has the distinction of having become the world's first national park in 1872. Since that time other countries have followed suit and have established their own national parks.

4 In the United States and its territories alone, there are more than 40 national parks, varying considerably in landscape and mood. Each park was chosen for its unique features, representative of a particular region of the country. Everglades National Park, for example, at the southern tip of Florida is a huge subtropical swamp, which provides refuge for such unusual reptiles as the alligator and for thousands of varieties of birds, including the graceful pink flamingo. In sharp contrast to the Everglades are the arid, dusty parks of the West. Mesa Verde National Park in Colorado, for example, preserves the ruins of an Indian civilization which flourished in the twelfth

and thirteenth centuries. Today, tourists can wander through the awesome cliff dwellings that the Indians carved out of the steep rock.

5 The National Park Service, a federal agency in charge of the parks, has two main functions. It must promote the parks and, at the same time, protect them from careless visitors. Obviously, it is difficult to achieve a balance between these two seemingly conflicting goals.

6 In the past, the Park Service focused on making the big scenic parks more accessible and comfortable for tourists. Roads were paved to allow "windshield visitors" to experience the grandeur of nature without leaving their cars, and a limited number of hotels and grocery stores were permitted to open within the park boundaries.

7 Now this trend is changing. Plans have been made to restore the parks to their natural condition as much as possible. The objective of such a move would be to ensure the preservation of the parks for future generations, while allowing present-day visitors to experience pure wilderness, free from any obvious signs of civilization—an opportunity which is rapidly disappearing in the twentieth century. Initial plans call only for a reduction in the number of cars allowed into the parks each day, but eventually, tourists may have to leave their cars at the gates and then either visit the park on foot or use park transportation. Additionally, stores and hotels may no longer be allowed within park boundaries and even the number of campgrounds may be restricted.

8 Denali National Park[1] in Alaska serves as an excellent model for this new type of park, one which has been changed only slightly from its natural state. There is only one road, unpaved in sections, which cuts through Denali. As car traffic is strictly limited, many visitors experience the magnifi-

cent scenery and wildlife from a park bus. There are no hotels or stores and only seven campgrounds within Denali's 3,000 square miles. This relative isolation offers backpackers, canoeists, and other sport enthusiasts a special physical and psychological challenge.

9   While the National Park Service has succeeded in protecting Denali's scenery and wildlife, it has been criticized for overlooking the promotional function of the organization. Critics feel that the national parks should continue to be made more accessible for visitors. In their opinion, the present policy to reduce or eliminate hotels, stores, and cars from within park boundaries may result in the exclusion of certain groups of park visitors, including families with children, senior citizens, and the handicapped.

10   Grand Canyon National Park in northern Arizona is at the center of this controversy. The canyon, carved by the powerful Colorado River, is 210 miles long, up to 18 miles wide and, in certain areas, one mile deep. Visitors to the canyon can experience it in several different ways. Some choose to journey from top to bottom on foot or on the back of a mule. Others prefer to view the canyon from the bottom looking up while navigating the white-water rapids[2] in the Colorado River on a rubber raft. Still others choose a bird's-eye view from the window of an airplane. All of these experiences, however, require time, money, or athletic ability. The fact is that the average tourist only peers over the rim of the canyon. Some people feel it is a shame that many visitors are restricted to this one perspective of the canyon. They propose installing a cable car to the bottom, making a trip down to the Colorado River and back up in a day possible. Opponents to this proposal feel that the effect on the canyon could be devastating.

11   These parks which were created to preserve areas of spectacular beauty in the United States are now being unintentionally threatened by those who come to admire them. To promote or to protect? This is the dilemma of the National Park Service. Perhaps the words of songwriter Joni Mitchell are worth bearing in mind:

"Don't it always seem to go
That you don't know what you've got
Till it's gone
They paved paradise
And put up a parking lot."[3]

Notes

1. Denali National Park: a park previously called Mount McKinley National Park after the tallest mountain in North America. It has since adopted the old Indian name for the 20,320-foot-tall mountain, "Denali," meaning "the High."
2. rapids: rough water created by rocks in a river.
3. From the song, "Big Yellow Taxi," by Joni Mitchell on Warner Brothers Records. © 1970 Siqoumb Publishing Corp. Used by permission. All rights reserved.

K. First Impressions

Do the following exercise without referring to the article. Circle the letter next to the statement that best answers the question.

1. Which of the following statements is false?
    a. The United States created the world's first national park in the late nineteenth century.
    b. Visitors still come to Yellowstone in the winter, although the park is closed.
    c. The "star" of Yellowstone is a geyser.
    d. There are national parks in United States territories.

2. What is the new philosophy of the National Park Service?
    a. To make the parks more comfortable for tourists.
    b. To promote their use.
    c. To protect the parks.
    d. To build more campsites for sport enthusiasts.

3. Grand Canyon National Park is a point of controversy because a number of people
    a. are afraid that the Colorado River is running dry.
    b. want to remove a cable car from the canyon.
    c. believe the park should have more roads, hotels, and stores.
    d. feel that the canyon should be made more accessible.

4. Denali National Park in Alaska
    a. is easily accessible for tourists.
    b. has a limited number of hotels and campgrounds.
    c. has only two roads for cars and buses.
    d. is relatively undeveloped.

5. Most tourists to the Grand Canyon
    a. take a mule ride.
    b. go for an airplane ride.
    c. stay at the top.
    d. walk to the bottom.
    e. all of the above.

L. Rapid Reading

Do this exercise in class. Scan the article quickly to find the following pieces of information. Write down the number of the paragraph in which each topic is discussed.

a. _____ the Grand Canyon

b. _____ Yellowstone in winter

c. _____ the past policy of the National Park Service

d. _____ Old Faithful

e. _____ the size of Denali National Park

f. _____ Mesa Verde

M. Between the Lines

Circle the letter next to the statement that best answers the question. You may refer to the text.

1. What is the main idea of paragraph 4?
   a. The large number of national parks.
   b. National parks as a wildlife refuge.
   c. The diversity of the national parks.
   d. The differences between Mesa Verde National Park and the Everglades.

2. "Windshield visitors" are tourists who
   a. seldom get out of their cars.
   b. stay in their cars to avoid the wind.
   c. wear large glasses for a better view.
   d. leave their cars in the park and walk.

3. In paragraph 9, sentence 1, the article states that the Park Service was criticized for overlooking one of its functions. In this context, "to overlook," means to
   a. supervise.
   b. ignore.
   c. look down upon.
   d. inspect.

4. In paragraph 4, sentence 4, "which" refers to
   a. Mesa Verde National Park.
   b. ruins.
   c. Indian.
   d. civilization.

5. From reading the last paragraph, it seems that Lisa
   a. does not care what happens to the national parks.
   b. believes parks should be easily accessible.
   c. feels parks should be more protected.
   d. feels that more parking lots are needed for visitors.

N. More Expressions

Fill in the blanks with words from the following list. Use the correct voice, tense, and singular or plural form of the noun.

unintentionally	outstanding	to ensure
to bear in mind	awesome	to peer
to follow suit	to flock	dilemma
	accessible	

1. Some of the dwellings in Mesa Verde are _____ only by ladder.

2. When visiting Yellowstone, it is wise _____ that the cute animals may be dangerous.

3. Visitors to the Grand Canyon are overwhelmed by the

    _____ view from the canyon's north rim.

4. The E.S.L. student at the University of Colorado at Boulder, was in

    a(n) _____ over how to spend his Christmas vacation. He could not decide whether to go home to Japan or spend two weeks skiing in the Rockies.

5. The West can boast of a number of _____ universities.

6. The man narrowed his eyes and _____ into the canyon, trying to spot the mule train at the bottom.

7. Every summer residents of Denver _____ to Red Rocks Theater for concerts under the stars.

8. The National Park Service _____ the safety of park visitors by providing sturdy railings at potentially dangerous spots.

9. A camper in Yellowstone who _____ leaves food out while he goes for a walk may return to find a hungry and dangerous grizzly bear having a feast.

10. A seagull flying over Great Salt Lake swooped down to catch a shrimp, and the rest of the flock immediately _____.

O. Express Yourself

1. a. Some friends who are going to visit a foreign country for the first time have asked you for advice. Help them by completing the following sentence:

   When visiting a foreign country it is important to *bear in mind* . . .
   b. The word "bear" has several meanings depending on its context. What does it mean in the following examples?

      a. to *bear* a heavy load.
      b. a brown *bear*.
      c. to *bear* a child.
      d. She couldn't *bear* seeing him again.

2. What is the *dilemma* of the United States government in regard to the land claims made by Native Americans?

3. People who are skilled in diplomacy, the art of negotiating between nations, are essential in world politics. Which current and former diplomats could be called *outstanding* and why?

4. How are "to *ensure*" and "to insure" similar? How are they different? Which of the following would you *ensure* and which would you insure?
   a. a car
   b. a future
   c. safety
   d. jewelry

P. Talk It Up

1. How did Old Faithful get its name?

2. How would you describe a "windshield visitor"?

3. The article mentions five ways in which visitors can experience the Grand Canyon. What are they?

4. What are some differences between Denali National Park and other national parks?

5. What is a "bird's-eye view"?

6. What are the two primary functions of the National Park Service? In your opinion, which is more important and why? Can the Park Service resolve its dilemma?

7. What do you think is the meaning of the lines by Joni Mitchell? Can you apply her message to experiences in your life?

Q. Word Families

Choose the appropriate form of the word. Be certain to use the correct verb tense, singular or plural form of the noun, and the passive voice where necessary.

1. isolation, to isolate, isolated
   a. People searching for _____ can find it in Montana's Glacier National Park.
   b. The rugged terrain _____ much of the park from the average tourist.
   c. Over 1000 miles of trails allow backpackers to hike to _____ lakes and snow-capped mountain peaks.

2. enthusiasm, enthusiast, enthusiastic, enthusiastically
   a. Skiing _____ come to Utah for dry, powdery snow and challenging slopes.

b. Their _____ for skiing often disappears, though, when the temperature drops below zero.

c. After one day of lessons and fun on the slopes, even beginners become _____ about skiing.

d. Expert skiers attack the steepest slopes _____ when the conditions are good.

3. variety, to vary, various
   a. Idaho is called the "Gem State" because of its wide _____ of gem stones, including opals, rubies, and emeralds.
   b. The state also has a wealth of _____ minerals.
   c. The landscape in Idaho _____ dramatically from gently rolling farmland to fantastic rock formations, such as those found in Craters of the Moon National Monument.

4. consideration, to consider, (in)considerate, considering, considerable, considerably
   a. At present several large companies _____ opening branch offices in Denver.
   b. A _____ number of data-processing companies have already moved there.
   c. Denver's population has grown _____ over the past few years.
   d. The city planning commission has had to take many factors into _____ when planning for the city's large scale growth.
   e. _____ its enormous growth in population, Denver has remained a very pleasant city.
   f. Visitors to the national parks are asked to be _____ of others and to clean up their litter carefully.

5. intention, to intend, (un)intentional, (un)intentionally
   a. It is the _____ of many foreign tourists to see all the national parks in the West.
   b. These tourists have _____ underestimated the size of the West and the distances between national parks.
   c. Better informed tourists _____ to take their time while traveling and visit only a few parks.
   d. The limited facilities in the national parks are _____; too many hotels and restaurants would spoil the natural beauty of the parks.

6. restriction, to restrict, restrictive, restricted
   a. The laws in the early days of the Wild West were not very _____.
   b. Few _____ were placed on the tough residents of mining and cattle towns.

c. Now hunting and fishing are not permitted in certain _____ areas.

d. Laws also _____ the use of guns in the West.

7. proposal, to propose, proposed

   a. A recent _____ has been made to control air pollution in Colorado.

   b. In a meeting held in Denver, the state capital, environmentalists _____ to limit the growth of polluting, heavy industries.

   c. The _____ plan would improve the quality of air in the foothills of the Rockies.

8. appreciation, to appreciate, appreciative

   a. To show her _____ for the excellent service, Lisa gave the waiter in the Boise restaurant a big tip.

   b. Many visitors to Dinosaur National Monument find it difficult _____ the fact that dinosaurs were alive 205 million years ago.

   c. As the weeks passed, Lisa became more and more _____ of her opportunity to become acquainted with the United States.

9. origin, to originate, original, originally

   a. Reno's reputation as a divorce capital _____ in the 1930s when a law was passed reducing the waiting period for a divorce to six weeks.

   b. _____ the waiting period was six months.

   c. Many of the lakes in the mountain states are of prehistoric _____.

   d. The present size of these lakes is much smaller than their _____ size.

10. creation, creativity, to create, creative, creatively

   a. The _____ of the western rodeo resulted from the every-day work of the cowboys.

   b. The challenge of taming a wild horse and roping a cow _____ the basis of the rodeo.

   c. Some cowboys, such as Charles Russell, were not only good cowhands but also _____ artists.

   d. Russell's paintings _____ portray life in the Wild West.

   e. Cowboys had to show _____ in finding entertainment on the trail. Some sang, others played cards, and still others shot at flies buzzing overhead.

R. Look It Up

1. Who was Buffalo Bill?

2. How did Yellowstone get its name?

3. What is a "rockhound" and why would he or she be interested in the state of Idaho?

4. How would you feel if someone shouted, "You hit the jackpot!"? What does the phrase "to hit the jackpot" mean?

5. What is a bristlecone and why is it particularly interesting?

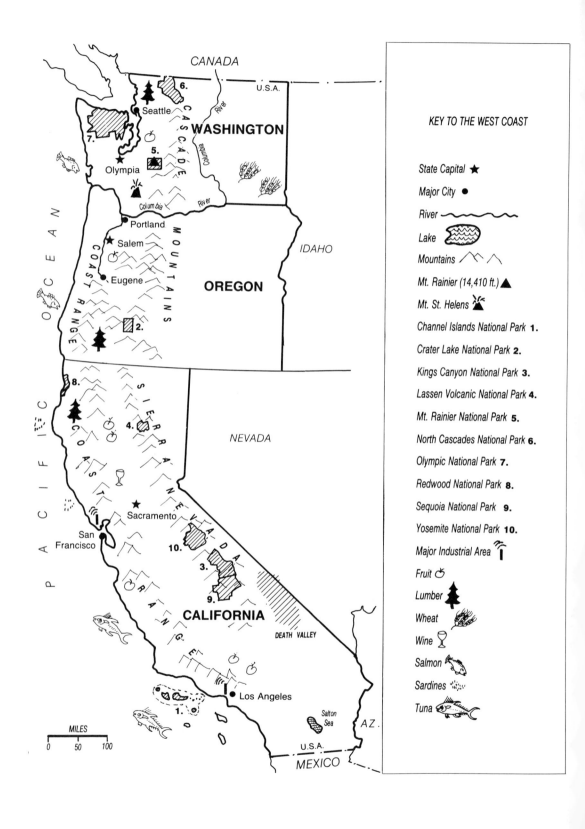

CANADA

U.S.A.

WASHINGTON

6.

Seattle

7.

CASCADE

5.

★ Olympia

Columbia River

Columbia River

Portland

★ Salem

MOUNTAINS

Eugene

OREGON

IDAHO

2.

COAST RANGE

PACIFIC OCEAN

8.

4.

SIERRA

NEVADA

NEVADA

★ Sacramento

San Francisco

10.

3.

9.

CALIFORNIA

COAST RANGE

DEATH VALLEY

Los Angeles

1.

Salton Sea

AZ.

MILES
0   50   100

U.S.A.

MEXICO

KEY TO THE WEST COAST

State Capital ★

Major City ●

River

Lake

Mountains

Mt. Rainier (14,410 ft.) ▲

Mt. St. Helens

Channel Islands National Park **1.**

Crater Lake National Park **2.**

Kings Canyon National Park **3.**

Lassen Volcanic National Park **4.**

Mt. Rainier National Park **5.**

North Cascades National Park **6.**

Olympic National Park **7.**

Redwood National Park **8.**

Sequoia National Park **9.**

Yosemite National Park **10.**

Major Industrial Area

Fruit

Lumber

Wheat

Wine

Salmon

Sardines

Tuna

chapter 9

The West Coast

A. Take a Look

I. Answer the following questions by looking at the map:

1. What is the capital of Washington?

2. Which river forms part of the boundary between Washington and Oregon?

3. Where is Sacramento located?

4. Which state has two O's in its name?

5. Which industries are common to all three states?

6. In which mountain range is Mount St. Helens located?

II. Make up questions that could be answered by the following information:

1. North Cascades, Olympic, and Mount Rainier

2. Salmon

3. Washington, Idaho, Nevada, and California

4. Salmon, tuna, and sardines

5. Sierra Nevada and Coast Range

B. A Letter from Lisa

Eugene, Oregon
August 7

Dear Steve,

Do you remember my friend Helen Parks, the one who used to work part-time for the advertising department of the <u>Daily</u>? Well, last January she was offered a job in the communications department of the University of Oregon. Within two weeks she had packed everything she owned and moved 3,000 miles across the country to Eugene, which is where I am right now, visiting Helen.

I can finally appreciate why she was so enthusiastic about moving out here. The countryside around Eugene is beautiful. It looks like a picture postcard with a vivid blue sky, endless, dark-green forests, and spectacular mountains in the distance. From Helen's office at the university I can see the Three Sisters, three peaks in the Cascades that are covered with snow all year long. I bet the skiing is fantastic here during the winter.

The gigantic fir trees are amazing, too. No wonder lumber is Oregon's leading industry. You could probably build a three-bedroom house with just one of these monstrous trees! But they do have their weak spots; the shallow depth of their roots is totally out of proportion with their towering height, so you can imagine what happens during a storm. As a matter of fact, last February one giant fir tree fell over, just barely missing Helen's neighbor's house! By the way, under no circumstances are the firs to be called pine trees. My terminology has been corrected several times already, but what can you expect from a woman raised in Maine, the "Pine Tree State"?

The weather has been excellent, just like I had always imagined it would be on the West Coast, with lots of warm, sunny days and no rain. Apparently it's not like this all the time though. There's a rainy season from November through February. When Helen first arrived in January, it rained for six days in a row. Now that I think of it, I remember speaking with her over the telephone at that time and hearing what I thought was someone taking a shower in the background—it was actually a rainstorm! If you think that's bad, just 250 miles north of here on the Olympic Peninsula, there's a rain forest which gets as much as 150 inches of precipitation a year! That means it must be constantly raining there! So don't ever complain about Boston's weather.

Helen has been a wonderful tour guide. We've been exploring Eugene with the enthusiasm of Lewis and Clark,[1] two well-respected heroes out here. We do most of our sightseeing on bicycles; Eugene has one of the most elaborate bike route systems in the country, with 150 miles of bike paths throughout the city. There are big, green signs to indicate the best routes to various places such as downtown or the university, making riding your bike here as easy as taking your car. In fact, it's even easier during rush hour. Best of all, the motorists respect the bicyclists, so accidents are rare. I wish all cities in the United States were as supportive of their cyclists as Eugene is. Then we could all ride our ten-speed bikes to work, conserve energy, save money, and get lots of exercise!

This afternoon Helen introduced me to another one of the local sports—tubing down the Willamette River. That means riding the rapids on an inner tube. At first I was petrified! I had no idea how to steer or stop, and I still don't! But I have to admit that once I got used to being out of control, it was really fun.

Tomorrow we're going on a little wine tour through the Willamette Valley, which stretches north to Portland. Helen claims that wine is an industry of the future in Oregon and maintains that someday wine from Oregon may be as common as wine from California. When I expressed my doubts, she informed me that the grape was Oregon's state flower—but she was referring to a plant that produces a cluster of berries that look like "normal" grapes but don't taste half as good! Speaking of fruit, there are "U-Pick-It"² signs everywhere for strawberries, cherries, and apples. To top it off, blackberries grow wild throughout the city, and right now just happens to be the beginning of the blackberry season. Yum!

It's been great visiting Oregon; I really like the attitude of the people here. They place a high value on the natural beauty of their state and work hard to preserve it. At the same time, lifestyles here, at least in Eugene, are more liberal, more relaxed. That must be why they say, "California hippies³ never grow old; they just move to Oregon!"

Take care and say hello to everyone at the <u>Daily</u> for me.

Love,

Lisa

Notes

1. Lewis and Clark: two explorers of the Northwest during the eighteenth century.
2. U-Pick-It: you pick the fruit yourself.
3. hippy: a term, popular in the 1960s, for a young person who has rejected the norms of society in favor of a more liberal lifestyle.

C. True or False?

Write T before those statements that are true and F before those that are false.

_____ 1. Fir tree is synonymous with pine tree.
_____ 2. Lumber is Oregon's number one industry.

_____ 3. The Three Sisters are really three mountains.
_____ 4. The branches of the fir tree are weak in spots.
_____ 5. Lisa had trouble controlling the inner tube.
_____ 6. Oregon's state flower is commonly used to make wine.
_____ 7. Helen Parks once worked for the same newspaper as Steve.
_____ 8. According to Helen Parks, wine from Oregon will someday be more common than wine from California.
_____ 9. The city of Eugene has made getting around town on a bicycle very simple.
_____ 10. The lifestyle in Eugene is best described as "conservative."

D. Close-up

Fill in the blanks with a, an, or the. If no article is necessary, put an X in the blank.

Eugene is _____ wonderful city, especially when seen from _____ seat
             (1)   (2)

of _____ bicycle—and there are _____ bicycles everywhere in Eugene!
   (3)   (4)

_____ first thing Lisa did when she arrived was to rent _____ ten-
 (5)   (6)

speed from one of _____ local bike shops. She was impressed by _____
                 (7)   (8)

quality of _____ bike route system in Eugene. _____ big, green signs
      (9)   (10)

indicated _____ fastest routes through town, so Lisa didn't even need
         (11)

_____ map of _____ city to get around. By _____ end of her stay,
 (12)   (13)   (14)

Lisa was totally familiar with Eugene and had become _____ expert
                                                       (15)

cyclist, too!

E. Expressions

Rewrite the following sentences, replacing the italicized words with the correct form of the appropriate word or expression.

to top it off	in a row	monstrous
elaborate	supportive	barely
no wonder	to bet	to steer
	petrified	

1. The young man was *hardly* able to catch up with the already moving San Francisco cable car, but he ran just a little faster and then hopped aboard.

2. Visitors to the West Coast often are not used to earthquakes and are *paralyzed with fear* if one happens to occur during their visit.

3. The General Sherman Tree, a giant sequoia measuring 275 feet (84 meters) in height and 103 feet (32 meters) in circumference, can only be described as *enormous*!

4. The San Diego Zoo is so beautiful that I *am sure* animals prefer living there in captivity to being free!

5. In Hollywood, the glamour capital of the world, you can see several very *complex* movie sets.

6. At Disneyland in Anaheim, Disney characters stand *one after the other* to greet you at the entrance.

7. Death Valley, which dips to 282 feet below sea level, and Mount Whitney, which climbs to 14,994 feet above sea level, are only 80 miles apart; *it's perfectly understandable why* California has been called a "state of extremes."

8. Helen's new home was ideal for her; it was small and comfortable, had a garden full of roses, and *to complete the picture*, was located just a five-minute bike ride from the university.

9. Helen's neighbor drives a huge logging truck. He has *to direct its course* up and down steep mountain roads. (Use "it" in your sentence.)

10. When Helen first moved to Eugene, she knew very little about the city, but her neighbors were *helpful* and gave her tips on how to get around, where to shop and so on.

F. Express Yourself

1. The most common meaning of *"to bet"* is "to wager," that is, "to put money on something." Do you like to *bet*? If so, what do you *bet* on? How do you think the colloquial meaning "to be sure" evolved?

2. Describe either your best or worst vacation and end your description with "*and to top it off . . .*"

3. When was the last time you were absolutely *petrified*? What happened?

G. Think Back

Answer the following questions according to the text.

1. Where did Lisa get to know Helen?

2. What are three sports mentioned in the letter that are popular in the Eugene area?

3. Why is the name of Oregon's state flower misleading?

4. What are some of the advantages of biking in Eugene instead of driving a car?

5. How does Lisa describe Oregon's residents?

H. Talk About It

1. Helen Parks did not hesitate to move 3,000 miles across the country to start a new job. Would you say her move is typical of "mobile" American society? Explain your answer. How would you feel about making such a move?

2. Is the bicycle a popular means of transportation in your native country? Are there any disadvantages to bicycle riding? What do you think about commuting to work on rollerskates and skateboards?

3. What are some popular sports in your hometown?

I. Words, Words, Words!

The following vocabulary items have been taken from Lisa's article. Try to guess the meaning of each word from the context and write your definition in the space provided. When you have finished, check the vocabulary list at the end of the book for the correct meaning.

1. abrasive _____
   Wind and *abrasive* sand damage the exteriors of homes on the northern California coast.

2. anticipate _____

The scientist, who had not *anticipated* any problems in finding the marine laboratory in Monterey, was sorry he had not brought a map.

3. blast _____

The *blast* from the gun echoed through the forest.

4. casualty _____

The airplane crash in the Sierra Nevadas resulted in five *casualties*.

5. collide _____

While walking through Seattle's Pike Street Market, the girl was so fascinated that she did not watch where she was going and *collided* with a man selling fresh fish.

6. core _____

Helen's brother-in-law, John, thinks that the *core* is the best part of the apple and he eats it, seeds and all!

7. debris _____

The devastating wind storm left a trail of *debris* in its path.

8. determined _____

Lisa was *determined* to finish her article before she left for the beach, so she went to her room to work.

9. drifting _____

Drifting down the Willamette River on a rubber raft is a nice, peaceful way to spend a summer afternoon.

10. engulf _____

A blanket of white fog *engulfed* the Golden Gate Bridge over San Francisco Bay.

11. long-awaited _____

Having run out of money, the student in San Diego was ecstatic when his *long-awaited* check from home finally arrived.

12. mutilated _____

After looking at the *mutilated* body of the plane, the rescue team was surprised that anyone had survived the crash.

13. overdue _____

When the busy student at Stanford University finally returned his library books, they were three weeks *overdue*.

Mt. St. Helens. A violent reminder that the earth is never still.

J. Headline

THE EARTH'S HIDDEN POWER COMES TO THE SURFACE

by Lisa Evans

1   "Vancouver! Vancouver! This is it!" The excited cry of young scientist, David Johnston, to his colleagues in Vancouver, Washington announced the long-awaited eruption of Mount St. Helens. These were David Johnston's last words. An instant later, his observation post six miles from the peak was engulfed by a wave of fiery hot gases and debris.

2   The eruption of Mount St. Helens in the southwestern corner of Washington on May 18, 1980, was equal in force to the largest hydrogen bomb ever tested. People in the Northwest had been anticipating an eruption for some time, but the blast was much bigger than expected. At 8:32 on a peaceful Sunday morning the mountain "blew its top." Clouds of gas, ash, and rock shot into

the air. As much as three inches of ash covered towns in Washington, Idaho, and Montana hundreds of miles away. The thick clouds of abrasive ash paralyzed regional car and air traffic and forced residents to stay inside or put on face masks. The blast leveled forests 17 miles away, and boiling mud flowed down the mountain's sides into neighboring rivers. As a result, the water temperature rose sharply from 50° to 90°F., causing fish to jump out of the hot water onto the banks. The eruption took the lives of 64 people in the vicinity of the mountain. Casualties included scientists, such as David Johnston, miners, loggers, determined residents, and curious tourists who had managed to evade protective roadblocks. The 200-square-mile area north of the mountain covered by a grey blanket of ash looked like a scene from a different planet.

3   The west coast of the United States is famous for its volcanic activity and earthquakes. Scientists have been trying to understand what powerful subterranean[1] forces can produce these dramatic acts of nature. One popular theory is known as continental drift, or ''plate tectonics.'' According to this theory, the surface of the earth is like the cracked shell of a soft-boiled egg. The outer crust of the earth is composed of pieces, called plates, which are about 60 miles thick and ''float'' on a semisolid core. These plates move very slowly, perhaps only a few inches per year; however, these small movements have large effects.

4   When the plates hit and grind against each other, earthquakes may occur. The San Andreas Fault, stretching 650 miles through southern and central California, forms the boundary between the Pacific Plate and the North American Plate. California regularly experiences earthquakes due to the shifting of these plates.

The quakes vary in strength. Some are so slight that they are noticeable only on a seismograph, an instrument which measures and records vibrations in the earth; whereas others are so powerful that they cause major property damage along the fault line. Most researchers agree that a major earthquake somewhere along the San Andreas Fault is long overdue; however, exactly when and where it will occur remains a mystery.

5   The drifting of the continental plates may also result in the creation of mountains and volcanoes. When two plates collide, one may slide under the other. As a result, the second plate is pushed up, forming mountain ranges such as the Cascades in Oregon and Washington. During this process the friction between the plates may produce enough heat to melt rock into magma. Volcanic eruptions occur when the magma is then forced up through cracks to the earth's surface.

6   Mount St. Helens is one of a chain of volcanoes in the Cascades. Scientists believe that the mountain's eruption may signal the awakening of other volcanoes in the chain. Oregon's Mount Hood, 60 miles southwest of Mount St. Helens, has shown signs of increased activity and is under careful watch. The question everyone in the Northwest is asking is ''What's next?'' No one can say for sure; however, it seems clear that the Cascade Range is capable of another performance at any time.

7   Meanwhile, life is returning to the slopes of Mount St. Helens. Little green shoots of hardy plants are pushing their way through the grey ash. Assuming there are no further major eruptions, in another century a new forest will have covered most of the mutilated landscape, leaving only a few reminders of the earth's hidden power.

Note

1. subterranean: beneath the earth's surface.

K. First Impressions

Do the following exercise without referring to the article. Circle the letter next to the statement that best answers the question.

1. The eruption of Mount St. Helens
   a. was a complete surprise.
   b. had been expected.
   c. did not cause extensive damage.

2. Which of the following statements is false?
   a. Earthquakes vary in size.
   b. The San Andreas Fault runs through southern and central California.
   c. Scientists can predict precisely when and where the next earthquake will occur.
   d. Another major earthquake is expected to occur in California.

3. The movement of the continental plates may produce
   a. earthquakes.
   b. mountains.
   c. volcanoes.
   d. both a and c.
   e. all of the above.

4. Which of the following were results of the eruption?
   a. People lost their lives.
   b. A layer of ash covered a 200-square-mile area north of the mountain.
   c. Forests 17 miles away were destroyed.
   d. Both a and c.
   e. All of the above.

5. After the eruption of Mount St. Helens
   a. no plants will ever grow in the immediate area again.
   b. people were advised to wait five to ten years before moving back to the area.
   c. plant life has already returned to the devastated area.
   d. fish had to learn how to live on river banks because the water temperature was too high.

L. Rapid Reading

Do this exercise in class. Scan the article quickly to find the following pieces of information. Write down the number of the paragraph in which each topic is discussed.

a. _____ the San Andreas Fault

b. _____ the process which causes volcanic eruptions

c. _____ the effects of Mount St. Helens' eruption

d. _____ the theory of continental drift

e. _____ the state of other volcanoes in the Cascades

M. Between the Lines

Circle the letter next to the statement that best answers the question. You may refer to the text.

1. In paragraph 2, sentence 3, the article states that the mountain blew its top. In this context, "blew its top" means
   a. got angry.
   b. erupted.
   c. created a windstorm.

2. In paragraph 3, sentence 2, the phrase "these dramatic acts of nature" refers to the events mentioned in
   a. paragraph 2, sentence 8.
   b. paragraph 3, sentence 1.
   c. paragraph 3, sentence 3.

3. In the article, the earth is compared to a soft-boiled egg because
   a. it is in a cooling period.
   b. its crust floats on a semisolid core.
   c. the underlying layer is white.

4. In paragraph 6, the article states that the eruption of Mount St. Helens may signal increased volcanic activity in the Cascades. In this context, "signal" means
   a. serve as an indication of.
   b. result in.
   c. put a stop to.

5. Paragraph 6 implies that
   a. all of the volcanoes in the Cascades will erupt sometime in the near future.
   b. further eruptions in the Cascade Range are unlikely.
   c. Mount Hood in Oregon could erupt in the near future.

6. Paragraph 1 implies that scientist David Johnston
   a. gave a complete report of the eruption to his colleagues.
   b. was killed by the eruption.
   c. suffered extensive burns on his body, but recovered from his injuries.

7. Within the context of paragraph 4, a "fault" is
   a. a mistake.
   b. a term used in tennis.
   c. a crack in the earth's crust.

N. More Expressions

Fill in the blanks with words from the following list. Use the correct voice, tense, and singular or plural form of the noun.

long-awaited   debris   determined
abrasive   to engulf   to drift
to anticipate   casualty   core
                   to collide

1. The small sailboat _____ by a large wave and almost sank.

2. Although Lisa and her cousin from Sacramento had been very close friends during childhood, they gradually _____ apart as they grew older.

3. The workers at Seattle's Boeing airplane plant admired their foreman's competence, but disliked his _____ personality.

4. The lumber companies in the Northwest, which were hurt by the drop in housing construction, felt that high interest rates were at the _____ of the problem.

5. The parents celebrated the _____ announcement of their daughter's engagement by taking everyone to dinner at the top of Seattle's Space Needle.

6. After squealing around the corner, the taxi _____ with a cable car.

7. The _____ climber wanted to reach the top of Mount Rainier by early afternoon.

8. The severe blizzard resulted in several _____ at the Lake Tahoe ski resort.

9. If you visit Oregon in the month of January, you can _____ several days of rainy weather.

10. After a large fir tree fell on their house during a storm, the owners needed several days to pull their belongings out from under the _____ .

O. Express Yourself

1. The end of the Vietnam War was a *long-awaited* event, as was the first landing of man on the moon. What are some other *long-awaited* events, both past and future?

2. What do you *anticipate* your life will be like in ten years? Where will you be living? What will you be doing?

3. It is a tradition for many people to start the year with a list of New Year's resolutions, that is, things they are *determined* to accomplish during the new year. Make a list of your goals for the upcoming months.

P. Talk It Up

1. What were some direct consequences of Mount St. Helens' eruption?

2. How can the drifting of the continental plates create mountains and volcanoes?

3. Why is Mount Hood under careful watch?

4. What kinds of major natural disasters has your native country experienced?

5. To what extent do you think man can control nature? Think back to previous chapters.

6. Communities with schools, hospitals, and business districts have been built directly on top of the San Andreas Fault. Earthquake and disaster experts agree that a major earthquake in the San Francisco area would undoubtedly result in thousands of deaths and billions of dollars in property damage. Why do people continue to live with such a potential danger in their backyard? Would you?

Q. Word Families

Choose the appropriate form of the word. Be certain to use the correct verb tense, singular or plural form of the noun, and the passive voice where necessary.

1. anticipation, to anticipate, anticipated
   a. The tour group's _____ departure date from San Francisco is August 24, but they might stay longer.
   b. In _____ of a rainy Oregon winter, the home owner decided to fix his leaky roof.
   c. If you go to Fisherman's Wharf in San Francisco on a Saturday afternoon, you can _____ seeing large numbers of people.

2. evasion, to evade, evasive
   a. When asked about the best place to fish on the Columbia, the man gave an _____ answer, not wanting to share his secret spot.

b. The company in Los Angeles had to pay a heavy fine for state income tax _____.

c. Not wanting to discuss politics with his father-in-law at dinner last night, the young man carefully _____ the issue of nuclear plants in northern California.

3. protection, protector, to protect, protective
   a. The federal government _____ the fishing and hunting rights of Native Americans in the Northwest.
   b. The cold campers on the Olympic Peninsula soon discovered that their little tent did not provide them with adequate _____ from the wind and rain.
   c. The two children were petrified of the sea lions because their parents had been too _____ of them around animals.
   d. The senator from Oregon was known as a _____ of the poor.

4. determination, to determine, determined
   a. After careful study, the authorities _____ that it was safe for people to return to their homes near Mount St. Helens.
   b. The E.S.L. students at the University of Oregon were _____ to speak English well before the end of the spring term.
   c. They succeeded in achieving their goal through sheer _____.

5. agreement, to agree, agreeable, agreeably
   a. The couple made an _____ to meet at the main gate of Disneyland at noon.
   b. The attendant at the gate answered _____ when they asked him for directions to the replica of a Mississippi paddlewheeler.
   c. The actress _____ to sign the contract for the new Hollywood movie only after she had read through it carefully.
   d. The new director of the American English Institute is a very _____, interesting person.

6. collision, to collide
   a. A waiter at Trader Vic's in downtown San Francisco _____ with a diner and almost dropped his tray.
   b. He was so embarrassed by the _____ that he turned bright red and disappeared into the restaurant's kitchen.

7. capability, capable, capably
   a. The graduate from the University of Washington was a very _____ computer programmer.
   b. A computer company in "Silicone Valley" near San Francisco recognized her _____ and offered her a job.
   c. She _____ wrote a complete software system for the company's new computer model.

8. expression, to express, expressive, expressionless
   a. When the poker player at the Lake Tahoe casino drew his fourth ace, his face remained _____.
   b. The crowd in the football stadium _____ its disappointment when the Oakland Raiders missed a touchdown.
   c. Lisa gave Helen a bouquet of flowers as an _____ of appreciation for her warm hospitality.
   d. The look that the father gave his 5-year-old daughter as she started to play with a very expensive vase in the Portland china shop was more _____ than words.

9. appearance, to appear, apparent, apparently
   a. Helen had improved the _____ of her house by painting it yellow with white trim.
   b. It _____ that nobody was home at Helen's because all the lights were off.
   c. Helen and Lisa had _____ gone out for the evening.
   d. To Lisa, there was no _____ difference between pine trees and fir trees, except for size.

10. theory, to theorize, theoretical, theoretically
    a. Researchers at the University of Oregon's Neuroscience Institute _____ about the central nervous system.
    b. The scientist gave a _____ explanation on how the brain functions.
    c. Most geologists accept the _____ the ocean once covered the region around Sequoia National Park.
    d. _____, Lisa's old Chevy is supposed to get 25 miles per gallon, but actually it gets only 20.

R. Look It Up

1. Who was Sacajawea and what role did she play in the Lewis and Clark expedition?

2. What happened during the San Francisco Earthquake of 1906?

3. What is a "forty-niner," and what does the phrase "to strike it rich" mean?

4. How was Crater Lake formed?

5. Refer to your map and find Death Valley. Why is it famous?

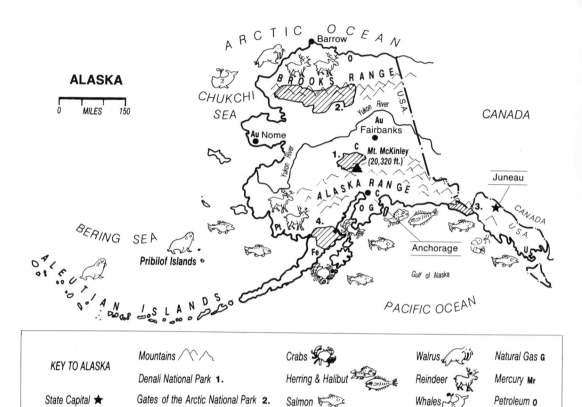

ALASKA

0 MILES 150

ARCTIC OCEAN

Barrow

CHUKCHI SEA

BROOKS RANGE

2.

Yukon River

U.S.A.

CANADA

Au Nome

Au Fairbanks

1. Mt. McKinley (20,320 ft.)

Juneau

ALASKA RANGE

3.

CANADA U.S.A.

Anchorage

BERING SEA

Pribilof Islands

4.

Fe

Gulf of Alaska

ALEUTIAN ISLANDS

PACIFIC OCEAN

KEY TO ALASKA	Mountains	Crabs	Walrus	Natural Gas G
	Denali National Park 1.	Herring & Halibut	Reindeer	Mercury Mr
State Capital ★	Gates of the Arctic National Park 2.	Salmon	Whales	Petroleum O
Major City ●	Glacier Bay National Park 3.	Shrimp	Gold Au Coal C	Platinum Pt
River	Katmai National Park 4.	Seals	Iron Fe	Uranium U

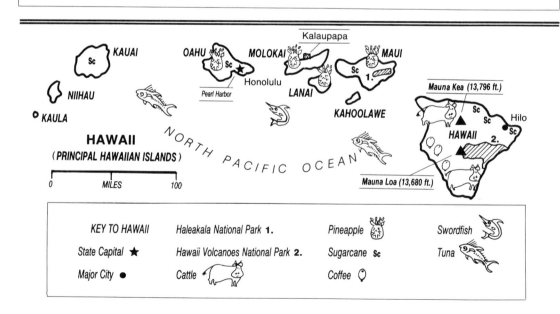

KAUAI

Sc

OAHU

Sc

MOLOKAI

Kalaupapa

MAUI

Sc

1.

Mauna Kea (13,796 ft.)

NIIHAU

Honolulu

Pearl Harbor

LANAI

Sc

KAHOOLAWE

HAWAII

Sc Sc

Hilo

Sc

KAULA

2.

HAWAII
(PRINCIPAL HAWAIIAN ISLANDS)

NORTH PACIFIC OCEAN

0 MILES 100

Mauna Loa (13,680 ft.)

KEY TO HAWAII	Haleakala National Park 1.	Pineapple	Swordfish
State Capital ★	Hawaii Volcanoes National Park 2.	Sugarcane Sc	Tuna
Major City ●	Cattle	Coffee	

chapter 10

The New Additions

A. Take a Look

I. Answer the following questions by looking at the map:

1. Which fish is a major industry in Alaska?

2. What are the two biggest industries on the Hawaiian Islands?

3. Where is Pearl Harbor?

4. What forms Alaska's northern border?

5. What are the names of Alaska's two mountain ranges?

6. On which Hawaiian islands are there national parks?

II. Make up questions that could be answered by the following information:

1. Honolulu

2. On the western edge of the biggest island

3. On the Pribilof Islands

4. Denali

5. West of Maui and south of Molokai

B. A Letter from Lisa

Honolulu, Hawaii
August 20

Dear Steve,

Aloha! In case you didn't already know, that's Hawaiian for welcome, hello, and good-bye. That's "welcome" to Hawaii for me, "hello" to you, and "good-bye" to my trip. In just a few more days, I fly back to Eugene to pick up my car (I left it at Helen's when I went to Alaska), and then it's straight back to Boston, back to my apartment, and back to the office. So this'll be my last letter to you, written about the last state on my itinerary and the last state to be added to the Union— Hawaii.

I'm staying on the island of Oahu, the "Gathering Place," at the home of two friends of mine from Maine, Sherry and Jon, a married couple who came here as tourists about eight years ago, fell in love with Hawaii, and then forgot to go home. Now they have jobs in Honolulu, live in a beautiful house right on the beach, and would never consider returning to the mainland for more than a visit. Their reason for staying is quite simple. As Sherry put it, "The way we see it, Hawaii is in technicolor and all the rest of the world is in black and white." After these past few months on the road, I've come to realize that each of the fifty states has its own special beauty and its own attractions for its inhabitants; otherwise, I might be inclined to agree wholeheartedly with her. No one can deny that Hawaii is a paradise with more than two thousand varieties of brilliantly colored tropical flowers, emerald beaches trimmed with white surf, and spectacular volcanic mountains, some of which are still active. And if that weren't enough to persuade you to stay, there's the added bonus of a subtropical climate, with an average temperature of 75° all year round. To top it all off, I learned that Hawaii has 13 state holidays—that's more than any other state in the country—so you even have extra time off from work to take advantage of living here!

As a matter of fact, about the only drawback Sherry and Jon could find to Hawaii, aside from the isolated location, was the high cost of living. Housing is expensive because Hawaii is a resort area, but then you can't expect a home in paradise to be cheap, can you? Gasoline is more expensive here than on the mainland because it has to be imported, but the bus system on Oahu is excellent, and the weather is conducive to getting around by bike or moped. Also, food prices are comparatively higher for those who prefer traditional American cuisine and shop in Oahu's air-conditioned supermarkets for canned and frozen goods imported from the mainland. But for those who are willing to try cooking "à la native," there are lots of farmers' markets like the one just down the beach, where Sherry does most of her shopping every Thursday. There, she gets fresh fish, vegetables, and exotic fruits like papayas, guavas, and coconuts, to name just a few, and everything is either caught or grown in Hawaii. I've become "addicted" to pineapple juice, the state's unofficial beverage, and to Hawaiian coffee, which, believe me, is out of this world!

Recreational activities are equally as varied and "native" as the food in Hawaii. A daily swim is taken for granted here and, of course, Hawaii boasts some of the most famous surfing spots in the world. Not being a surfer, I stuck to riding the waves in an outrigger canoe[1] (really fun!) and to learning to dance the hula.[2] Between West Virginian clogging and the Hawaiian hula, I now have quite a dance repertoire, wouldn't you say?

Here's another interesting fact on Hawaii that I'll bet you never knew. If you live in Rutland, you're a Vermonter, and if you reside in Cheyenne, you're a Wyomingite. If your hometown's Topeka, you're considered a Kansan, but what are you if you're from Honolulu? You're an "islander," and chances are good that you're not Hawaiian, a term which refers only to those whose ancestry can be traced back to the original settlers from Polynesia. Actually, there are very few pure Hawaiians left, except on the island of Niihau where there is an ancient Hawaiian community. I'm sorry to say that it's off-limits to tourists.

There was a time, less than 200 years ago, when all the islands were populated by pure Hawaiians, and the only "non-natives" around were sailors from whaling and trading ships anchored offshore. The Hawaiians were still a pagan[3] people ruled by the "alii," the noble class which cultivated fat as a royal status symbol. (Obviously, it wasn't "in" to be thin back then!) Human sacrifices to the gods of nature such as Pele, goddess of volcanoes, were an accepted part of the Hawaiian way of life. Then, in 1820, missionaries[4] from New England arrived, determined to save the natives from their pagan ways by introducing them to Christianity. Some of these missionaries stayed on in Hawaii for less altruistic reasons. They were the ones who started many of Hawaii's present business empires, notably its pineapple and sugarcane industries. When workers were needed in the fields of their plantations, Chinese, and then Japanese, laborers were brought to the Hawaiian Islands. Since then, Koreans, Puerto Ricans, Filipinos, and disenchanted twentieth century mainlanders, like Sherry and Jon, have added themselves to the multicultural mixture of islanders. The result is a "rare species" of people with the optimism and drive of the United States, mellowed by the serenity and gentleness of Polynesia and the Orient. They're also a people who love to party. I'm invited to a luau[5] this evening and it should be a good time!

I'm looking forward to seeing you and everyone else at work soon. But let me warn you, I've taken ten rolls of colored film. That's 360 slides, and I intend to show you every single one, so be prepared for a long evening! Then again, I'm a journalist, not a photographer, so if you're lucky, there might be a few that didn't turn out.

Aloha!

Lisa

Notes

1. outrigger canoe: a canoe with a log attached to one side to prevent it from overturning.
2. hula: a graceful Polynesian dance characterized by rhythmic movements of the hips and hands.
3. pagan: referring to people who worship many gods.
4. missionaries: people who work to spread a religious belief and/or carry out humanitarian work.
5. luau: a Hawaiian feast characterized by native dishes and entertainment.

C. True or False?

Write T before those statements that are true and F before those that are false.

_____ 1. In just a few more days, Lisa is flying back to Boston.

_____ 2. According to Sherry, Hawaii is the most colorful spot in the world.

_____ 3. The only drawback to living in Hawaii mentioned in the letter is the high cost of living.

_____ 4. The mountains of Hawaii are all active volcanoes.

_____ 5. The people of Hawaii are called islanders.

_____ 6. The missionaries to Hawaii were from the northeastern part of the United States.

_____ 7. Lisa learned to dance the luau in Hawaii.

_____ 8. Sherry and Jon refuse to return to the mainland, even for a visit.

_____ 9. If you want to see an ancient Hawaiian community, you can easily visit the island of Niihau.

_____ 10. Less than 200 years ago, human sacrifices were still taking place in Hawaii.

D. Close-up

Fill in the blanks with the appropriate preposition.

It wasn't until 1959 that Hawaii, located 2000 miles _____ the coast
                                                    (1)

_____ California, became the fiftieth state. _____ all, there are 122
  (2)   (3)

Hawaiian Islands, stretching _____ a line more than 1500 miles long.
(4)

Probably the most infamous _____ the islands is Molokai, the Friendly
(5)

Isle, _____ which Hawaiian monarchs first exiled those _____ the
(6)   (7)

dreaded disease, leprosy, _____ the 19th century. Today only a part
(8)

_____ Molokai is still a leper colony, Kalaupapa, where people continue
(9)

to be treated _____ the disease but _____ much better conditions than
(10)   (11)

before. As yet, there is no guaranteed cure, and because leprosy is so highly

contagious, children are a rare sight _____ Kalaupapa Leper Colony.
(12)

Pregnant women _____ the colony, whether suffering _____ leprosy
(13)   (14)

themselves or living there because _____ their husbands, must go
(15)

_____ another island _____ the birth _____ their children. After the
(16)   (17)   (18)

birth, women _____ leprosy return _____ Molokai _____ further
(19)   (20)   (21)

treatment. The others must choose _____ remaining _____ their
(22)   (23)

children or returning _____ their husbands.
(24)

E. Expressions

Rewrite the following sentences, replacing the italicized words with the correct form of the appropriate word or expression.

wholeheartedly	out of this world	to mellow
altruistic	to be conducive to	bonus
off-limits	repertoire	drawback
	to harbor	

1. Besides the experience of panning for gold, a tour of the Juneau Gold Mine in Alaska might offer you an *additional advantage*—you could find a gold nugget!

2. In order to protect its wildlife, Denali National Park is *closed* to tourist cars; however, free shuttle bus service is available for park visitors.

3. For those who enjoy seafood, tasting Alaskan king crab is a "must"—it's *superb*!

4. The Pacific Ocean around the Hawaiian Islands *is the home of* many varieties of tropical fish.

5. Lower off-season hotel rates *promote* tourism during Hawaii's rainy months.

6. The major *disadvantage* to vacationing in the Hawaiian Islands is that eventually you have to go home.

7. The majority of Japanese and Chinese immigrants to Hawaii adopted their new home *with total commitment.*

8. After dinner, Lisa and her friends went to a Don Ho concert, during which he sang several favorites from his *program of songs.*

9. Father Damien, the famous priest who did so much to improve conditions in the leper colony on Molokai, was poorly rewarded for his *selfless* actions; he contracted leprosy and subsequently died of it.

10. The normally tense businessman *was relaxed* by the gentle breeze and warm sand of Waikiki Beach.

F. Express Yourself

1. Can you think of any famous people who merit being called *altruists*? It has also been said that there is no such thing as a true *altruist,* a totally unselfish person. Do you agree or disagree with this statement? Explain your answer.

2. Which places mentioned in Lisa's letters from Utah and Florida were *off-limits* to the average tourist? Think of some other places that would have an *off-limits* sign on the door or at the entrance.

3. What are some of the drawbacks of the following?
   a. being married/single
   b. living in a foreign country
   c. being famous
   d. being a student

G. Think Back

Answer the following questions according to the text.

1. How did the following groups end up in Hawaii: Japanese and Chinese? New Englanders?

2. Give some of the reasons why Lisa considers Hawaii a paradise.

3. What people originally settled the Hawaiian Islands and what were they like?

4. What examples did Lisa give of Hawaii's high cost of living?

5. How does Lisa describe the character of the "islanders"?

H. Talk About It

1. Describe a place you have visited or would like to visit that you consider to be a paradise. Explain your choice.

2. What are shopping habits like in your native country? Where do people shop for food and how often?

3. What is the ethnic makeup of your native country and how did it come about?

I. Words, Words, Words!

The following vocabulary items have been taken from Lisa's article. Try to guess the meaning of each word from the context and write your definition in the space provided. When you have finished, check the vocabulary list at the end of the book for the correct meaning.

1. absurd _____
   To bring a winter coat to Honolulu would be *absurd;* the temperature is always moderate.

2. disregard _____
   The tourist from Oregon on the beach at Waikiki *disregarded* warnings to be careful of the sun and ended up with a painful sunburn.

3. drastic _____
   There had been a *drastic* change in the gold miner's appearance during the winter in the Alaskan wilderness; his hair had turned completely gray and he had lost at least 50 pounds.

4. durable _____
   The clothing made by Eskimos out of animal hide was not only warm but *durable;* it would last for years.

5. encroaching _____
   The gradually *encroaching* jungle slowly covered the ruins of the ancient Hawaiian temple.

6. eradication _____
   Since the *eradication* of mosquitos is impossible, backpackers in the Alaskan wilderness should come prepared with a good insect repellent and mosquito netting.

7. indiscriminately _____
   Wanting to charter a boat, but unfamiliar with the available companies, the fisherman *indiscriminately* chose a company from the Nome telephone book.

8. lull _____
   During the humid month of August there is a relative *lull* in Hawaii's tourist trade.

9. revival _____
   Increased tourism resulted in a *revival* of interest among Eskimos in pursuing their native arts and crafts.

10. roam _____
    Grizzly bears, which can reach seven feet in height, *roam* freely through the forests of Denali National Park.

11. sleek _____
    After a good brushing, the dog's fur was *sleek* and shiny.

12. stringent _____
    Not everyone can meet the *stringent* requirements of life in the Arctic.

Greenpeace members attempting to stop a foreign whaling vessel.

J. Headline

SAVE OUR SEALS AND WHALES
by Lisa Evans

1   As spring comes to the rough Bering Sea and the gigantic ice floes begin to melt, the water becomes alive with migrating animals. Both whales, the graceful giants of the deep, and sleek, gray seals can be seen swimming northward through narrow channels in the shifting ice. These animals, which have long been threatened by encroaching civilization, may soon disappear from the Bering and other seas around the world unless protective measures are taken.

2   For centuries whales, intelligent, air-

breathing mammals, were abundant in the waters off the Alaskan coast; however, their isolated sanctuary was invaded by hunters in 1848 when an American whaling ship discovered the rich whaling area. During the next 60 years, whalers, in search of bone and oil, almost destroyed the entire whale population of the Bering Sea. Particularly harmed by the unrestricted commercial whaling were the slow-moving bowhead whales; so many of them were killed that the species never recovered. At present, the population of the bowhead is estimated at less than 3,000. According to many conservationists, it is the most endangered whale on earth.

3   In an attempt to avoid the eradication of other whale species, countries interested in commercial whaling established the International Whaling Commission (IWC) in 1946. The IWC limits the number of whales that may be killed per year, and since 1973 the Commission has been steadily reducing its quotas. Today, only about seven countries still engage in commercial whaling. The reductions recommended by the IWC have brought loud cries of protest from countries with large whaling industries, especially Japan and the Soviet Union. These countries fear that their industries will not be able to survive such drastic cuts and that their national economies will suffer as a result. Although the IWC has no means of enforcing its regulations, since most whaling takes place in international waters, the Japanese and the Soviets are reluctant to ignore them. Previous decisions to disregard whale quotas resulted in costly boycotts of Japanese and Russian products by American conservationists.

4   The IWC would like to ban hunting of the endangered bowhead; however, this proposal has created a great deal of controversy in the United States due to strong protests from Alaskan Eskimos. The natives of Alaska resent the attempt to take away their hunting rights. For over 1,000 years, they have depended upon whales for the meat and raw materials necessary for survival in the Arctic. Present United States laws already strictly limit the number of whales that may be killed by each village; nevertheless, the population of the bowhead whale is critically low—perhaps too low to survive even minimal hunting by the Eskimos.

5   Another animal of the Bering Sea that is faced with possible extinction is the northern fur seal, valued highly by hunters for its soft and durable fur. The Pribilof Islands, 200 miles north of the Aleutian Islands off the Alaskan coast, are the seal's summer breeding grounds. For centuries the isolated islands have been the annual goal for thousands of migrating fur seals, some coming from as far south as the waters off southern California. The seals were undisturbed by humans until 1786 when the islands were discovered by Gerasim Pribilof, a Russian fur trader. Recognizing the potential profit, Pribilof immediately sent his men ashore with orders to kill as many seals as they could skin during the summer. Over the next fifty years, Russian hunters proceeded to kill an estimated 80 percent of the northern fur seal population, reducing to about 600,000 a herd that had probably numbered close to 3 million. This mass slaughter did not stop until the herd had decreased to the point where commercial hunting was no longer profitable.

6   During the subsequent lull in hunting, the seal population made a good, although temporary, recovery. By the time the United States bought Alaska, including the Pribilof Islands, from Russia in 1867, the seal herd had increased to around 2.5 million. This recovery resulted in a revival of hunting on the islands and at sea; however, fur hunters from around the world shot at

the animals indiscriminately, killing even pregnant and nursing females, and once again the species neared extinction.

7   In 1911, only 200,000 seals remained when the United States, Japan, Russia, and Canada signed a treaty that forbade the killing of female seals. The agreement, which is still being followed today, saved the northern fur seal from immediate extinction.

8   In the United States, a growing public awareness of these endangered species has caused a drop in the demand for seal fur and a ban on the importation of whale products; nevertheless, this spring hunters around the world will kill thousands of seals and whales. The furs of the seals will appear in stores as sealskin coats and gloves, and the whales will be transformed into such diverse products as steaks, soap, pet food, glue, crayons, and suntan lotion. Concerned individuals and conservationist groups, such as Greenpeace, continue to argue that it is absurd to use endangered species for such products, especially when suitable alternatives exist. Consequently, they are demanding that further restrictions be imposed on whale and seal hunting in the hopes that the 200-year exploitation of these animals by civilization will come to an end and that seals and whales will once again be allowed to roam the seas undisturbed.

K. First Impressions

Do the following exercise without referring to the article. Circle the letter next to the statement that best answers the question.

1. Which of the following statements is false?
   a. The number of countries involved in commercial whaling has decreased.
   b. The IWC has been steadily increasing its quotas.
   c. Japan and the Soviet Union do not support large cuts in whale quotas.
   d. The IWC permits a certain number of whales to be killed per year.

2. According to the article, why do Japan and the Soviet Union hesitate to disregard the IWC regulations?
   a. They want to preserve endangered species.
   b. The IWC strictly enforces its regulations.
   c. Public pressure in the United States has had serious consequences.
   d. Their national economies are dependent upon whaling.

3. Which of the following statements is true?
   a. Present United States laws do not restrict hunting of the bowhead whale.
   b. The bowhead whale is a new source of food for Eskimos.
   c. It took many years before the bowhead whale completely recovered from its initial slaughter.
   d. Minimal hunting may be devastating for the bowhead whale.

4. The Pribilof Islands
   a. are the year-round home of the northern fur seal.
   b. were discovered by a Russian whaling ship.
   c. are off the coast of southern California.
   d. were previously owned by Russia.

5. The treaty signed in 1911 regarding the northern fur seal
   a. is no longer being followed.
   b. restricts seal hunting.
   c. resulted in the near extinction of the fur seal.
   d. bans seal hunting.

L. Rapid Reading

Do this exercise in class. Scan the article quickly to find the following pieces of information. Write down the number of the paragraph in which each topic is discussed.

a. _____ Eskimos

b. _____ Greenpeace

c. _____ establishment of the IWC

d. _____ the first large whaling ship in the Bering

e. _____ the purchase of Alaska

f. _____ the discovery of the Pribilof Islands

M. Between the Lines

Circle the letter next to the statement that best answers the question. You may refer to the text.

1. The main idea of the article is
   a. the consequences of whaling in Alaska.
   b. how man has endangered seals and whales.
   c. seal hunting on the Pribilof Islands.
   d. Alaskan wildlife.

2. In paragraph 2, the article implies that a large number of bowhead whales were killed in the nineteenth century because
   a. they were abundant in the Bering Sea.
   b. their oil and bones are particularly valuable.
   c. they are slow swimmers.
   d. they are bigger and, therefore, better targets.

3. In paragraph 3, sentence 4, "protest" is pronounced
   a. pro test'
   b. pro' test

4. In paragraph 6, sentence 1, the word "subsequent" means
   a. following.
   b. next.
   c. temporary.
   d. important.

5. In the phrase, "to impose restrictions," as used in paragraph 8, the verb "impose" means
   a. remove.
   b. relax.
   c. invalidate.
   d. establish.

N. More Expressions

Fill in the blanks with words from the following list. Use the correct voice, tense, and singular or plural form of the noun.

encroaching	lull	indiscriminately
absurd	to roam	eradication
to disregard	drastic	revival
	stringent	

1. Over the past decade, the _____ ocean has washed away several feet of Oahu's shoreline.

2. Inconsiderate campers who _____ park regulations may be asked to leave Haleakala National Park.

3. In a hurry to leave for an island tour, Lisa _____ grabbed one of her notebooks.

4. Climbing Mount McKinley is a(n) _____ test of a mountain climber's skill and daring.

5. During a(n) _____ in conversation at the luau, Lisa went to get herself another piece of fresh papaya.

6. After several weeks of cool and cloudy weather the bright sun and warm temperatures resulted in a _____ of surfing.

7. Having spent a perfect day on Kauai, the "Garden Isle," Lisa almost did something _____. She considered calling Steve to tell him she was quitting her job and staying in Hawaii.

8. To go to Alaska in the winter time without mittens is

_____.

9. Alaska's National Wildlife Refuges protect animals from possible

_____.

10. With heads bent downward, beachcombers _____ the shoreline seeking shells and other treasures from the ocean depths.

O. Express Yourself

1. It is *absurd* to
   a. expect to learn English in three days!
   b. swallow live goldfish!
   c. try to fit ten people in a Volkswagen bug!
      What are at least five more *absurdities*?

2. Which of the following would *you* choose *indiscriminately*? Why would you be more *discriminating* in your other choices?
   a. a friend
   b. clothes
   c. a thumbtack
   d. a pencil
   e. a book

3. What would be a *drastic* way to do the following? A moderate way?
   a. quit smoking
   b. fix a toothache
   c. settle an argument
   d. lose weight

P. Talk It Up

1. What is the primary purpose of the IWC?

2. Why can't the IWC enforce its regulations?

3. What effect has public opinion in the United States had on the United States market for seal fur and whale products?

4. What dilemma does the United States government face in regard to the bowhead whale and the Eskimos?

5. In what ways might oil exploration in northern waters affect regional whale and seal populations?

Q. Word Families

Choose the appropriate form of the word. Be certain to use the correct verb tense, singular or plural form of the noun, and the passive voice where necessary.

1. reluctance, reluctant, reluctantly
   a. Lisa was a little _____ to end her trip and return to Boston.
   b. She waved good-bye _____ to her friends at the Honolulu airport.
   c. Her _____ was quickly replaced by anticipation, though, when she boarded the plane for the West Coast.

2. diversity, to diversify, diverse
   a. On her return flight across the Pacific, Lisa contemplated the _____ people and places she had become acquainted with during the past three months.
   b. At the start of her trip she had been unaware of the _____ found across the United States.
   c. Not wanting its economy to become overly dependent upon oil drilling, Alaska is trying _____ its business interests.

3. optimism, optimist, optimistic, optimistically
   a. Filled with glowing _____, people flocked to Alaska around the turn of the century to seek their fortune in gold mining.
   b. They were all very _____ about their chances of striking it rich.
   c. Many of the previously enthusiastic _____ became discouraged and gave up after several months of back-breaking work with no reward.
   d. Present-day visitors to the Juneau Gold Mine _____ search through the sand for a trace of gold.

4. serenity, serene, serenely
   a. Visitors to the island of Hawaii can forget their cares on _____, sheltered beaches.
   b. Palm trees _____ wave in cool ocean breezes.
   c. The island's _____ is only occasionally broken by eruptions from its volcanoes.

5. expectation, to expect, expectant, expectantly
   a. Having heard about Glacier National Park, the passengers on the ship cruising along the Alaskan coast _____ to see a number of glaciers and icebergs.
   b. Everyone was _____ standing at the ship's railing.
   c. The _____ passengers were trying to spot their first iceberg in the water.
   d. Their _____ were fulfilled when the ship rounded a bend and magnificent Glacier Bay came into view.

6. imposition, to impose, imposing
   a. Not wanting _____ upon a "friend of a friend" in Fairbanks, Lisa initially got a room at a hotel.
   b. Repeating that Lisa would be no _____, the friend of a friend insisted that she stay with her.
   c. Mount McKinley, the tallest mountain in North America, is an _____ sight as it towers over Denali National Park.

7. expense, to expend, expensive, expendable
   a. Lisa was afraid that while she was away Steve would decide that she was _____.
   b. Most of Lisa's travel _____ were covered by the *Daily*.
   c. Sled dog racing is an _____ Alaskan sport.
   d. The valuable huskies and their drivers _____ great amounts of energy racing the sleds over snow-covered paths.

8. rarity, rare, rarely
   a. In the Arctic, the summer temperature _____ exceeds 40°F. (5°C.).
   b. The Alaskan wilderness harbors many _____ species of delicate wild flowers.
   c. Since roads are a _____, most travel in northern Alaska is by plane.

9. excellence, to excel, excellent, excellently
   a. While in Anchorage, Lisa went to a restaurant which was well known for the _____ of its seafood.
   b. For dinner she ordered Alaskan king crab that was _____ prepared.
   c. The natives of many villages in Alaska _____ in the art of basket weaving.

d. Their _____ craftsmanship can be clearly seen in the intricately woven baskets.

10. symbol, to symbolize, symbolic, symbolically
    a. The Hawaiian lei, a necklace of fragrant flowers, is often a _____ of peace and goodwill.
    b. In the hula, graceful hip movements are accompanied by _____ hand gestures.
    c. The gestures _____ many aspects of nature, including ocean waves and sea breezes.
    d. Dancers in grass skirts move _____ to music played on native Hawaiian instruments.

R. Look It Up

1. What was Seward's Folly?

2. How many islands make up the chain of the Hawaiian Islands? How were the islands formed?

3. What is scrimshaw?

4. Who were called "sourdoughs" and how did they get their name?

5. Look up some information on the Alaskan Eskimos. For example, what was their lifestyle like previously and how has it changed?

6. Greenpeace is a very active international conservationist group. Look up information in the library or call or write the nearest chapter to find out what they have been doing to protect whales and seals around the world.

LISA'S TRACKS ACROSS THE U.S.A.

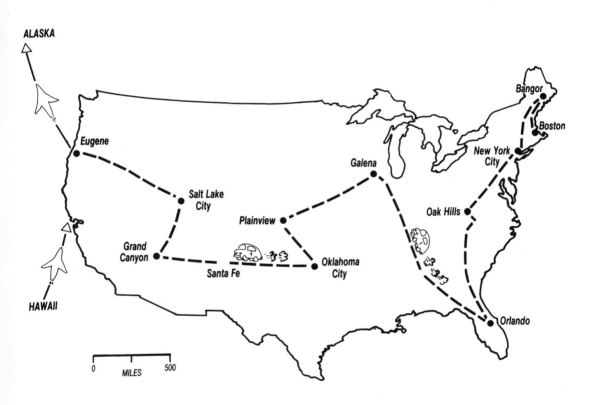

Appendices

Vocabulary List

The following vocabulary items have been used in section **I. Words, Words, Words!** *The chapter number is the chapter in which the word first appears.*

A

abrasive rough, irritating; Ch. 9
absurd ridiculous; Ch. 10
abundance a large quantity of something; Ch. 7
accessible possible to reach; Ch. 8
advocate a person who supports a cause; Ch. 3
ambivalent not being able to decide between alternatives; Ch. 6
anticipate to expect; Ch. 9
arid very dry; Ch. 6
awesome overwhelming; Ch. 8

B

ban to prohibit; Ch. 1
bar to keep out; Ch. 4
bear in mind to remember; Ch. 8
blast explosion; Ch. 9
brandish to wave angrily; Ch. 4

C

casualty a person who has been killed or seriously injured in a disaster; Ch. 9
challenge a test of a person's skill or knowledge; Ch. 3
collide to run into something; Ch. 9
compensate to make up for; Ch. 5
compromise an agreement in which each party has had to give up something; Ch. 7
consumption the process of using something up; Ch. 3
contaminate to pollute; Ch. 4
controversial arousing opposing opinions; Ch. 2
conversion the process of changing something into something else; Ch. 2
core the center of something; Ch. 9
cut down on to decrease; Ch. 3

D

debris the remains of something that has been destroyed; Ch. 9

defect a fault; Ch. 5

degenerate to worsen; Ch. 6

deplete to use up; Ch. 5

deplorable extremely bad; Ch. 6

despair the loss of hope; Ch. 6

determined wanting to accomplish something very much, resolved; Ch. 9

devastating very destructive; Ch. 5

dilapidated in bad condition; Ch. 1

dilemma a situation involving a decision between unsatisfactory choices; Ch. 8

disarm to take away someone's weapons; Ch. 6

discrepancy difference; Ch. 4

discrimination unfair treatment on the basis of a certain characteristic; Ch. 4

disposal the process of getting rid of something; Ch. 2

disregard to ignore; Ch. 10

doomed certain to fail or be destroyed; Ch. 6

drastic having a strong effect; harsh, severe, or extreme; Ch. 10

drifting moving slowly; Ch. 9

drowsiness sleepiness; Ch. 3

duplicate to copy; Ch. 1

durable able to withstand a lot of use; Ch. 10

dwelling a house; Ch. 8

dwindle to decrease gradually; Ch. 7

E

encroaching moving forward beyond the usual limits; Ch. 10

engulf to overwhelm; Ch. 9

ensure to guarantee; Ch. 8

enterprising willing to experiment and undertake new projects, usually in business; Ch. 1

eradication getting rid of something completely; Ch. 10

evacuate to leave a place because of danger; Ch. 2

evaporate to change into vapor; Ch. 7

extended longer; Ch. 2

extensive more than average in size or amount; Ch. 2

extinction disappearance; Ch. 1

F

face to have before oneself a difficult or unpleasant possibility; Ch. 7

feat an amazing act; Ch. 5

flock to come in large numbers; Ch. 8

flourish to grow or do well; Ch. 5

follow suit to follow someone's example; Ch. 8

foster to encourage; Ch. 6

G

gossip talk that may or may not be true; Ch. 1

H

harsh severe; Ch. 6

heightened increased; Ch 4

hostile unfriendly; Ch. 6

I

indiscriminately randomly; Ch. 10

ineligible not qualified; Ch. 4

initially at first; Ch. 6

innovation a new idea, method, or device; Ch. 5

K

keep up with to stay informed; Ch. 5

L

layout physical arrangement; Ch. 1

lethal deadly; Ch. 2

linger to stay for a while; Ch. 1

link connection; Ch. 3

long-awaited expected for a long time; Ch. 9

lucrative profitable; Ch. 3

lull a temporary quiet period; Ch. 10

M

merely only; Ch. 1

mighty powerful; Ch. 7

mutilated destroyed or severely injured; Ch. 9

N

nickname a more personal, often more descriptive name; Ch. 1

nontoxic not poisonous; Ch. 3

O

offspring the young of an animal; Ch. 5

outcome result; Ch. 2
outstanding exceptionally good; Ch. 8
overdue late in respect to a specified time; Ch. 9

P

peer to look curiously at something; Ch. 8
persist to continue; Ch. 4
plight a bad state or condition; Ch. 6
portray to describe; Ch. 6
postpone to put off until a later time; Ch. 2
potentially possibly; Ch. 2
preach to speak out strongly on a subject; Ch. 4
propel to push; Ch. 6
proponent supporter; Ch. 1

Q

quit to stop; Ch. 3

R

rare uncommon; Ch. 4
remarkable amazing; Ch. 5
remote far away; Ch. 2
replenish to fill again; Ch. 5
replica a reproduction; Ch. 1
resemble to look like; Ch. 2
reserve supply; Ch. 5
revival a period of renewed activity; Ch. 10
risky possibly dangerous; Ch. 2

roam to wander; Ch. 10
run out of to have no more of something; Ch. 7

S

sacrifice to give up something; Ch. 7
segregated separated according to a certain characteristic; Ch. 4
self-esteem self-respect; Ch. 6
sensible reasonable; Ch. 2
shortage an insufficient supply; Ch. 7
sleek smooth; Ch. 10
spoil to ruin; Ch. 2
stringent strict; Ch. 10
struggle fight; Ch. 4
substantial large; Ch. 1
survive to remain alive; Ch. 7
sustain to maintain; Ch. 5
symptom a sign that indicates the presence of an illness; Ch. 3

T

take for granted not to appreciate something fully because one is accustomed to it; Ch. 7
trait characteristic; Ch. 5

U

unaware having no knowledge of; Ch. 3
undergo to experience; Ch. 5
unintentionally accidentally; Ch. 8

Answer Key

Chapter 1:

C. 1. T 2. F 3. T 4. T 5. F 6. T 7. T 8. F 9. T 10. F **D.** 1. an 2. X 3. the 4. the 5. the 6. the 7. X 8. X 9. X 10. a 11. the 12. a 13. X 14. the 15. the **E.** 1. fitting 2. fade 3. numb 4. littering 5. grumbling 6. chunks 7. unbearable 8. innumerable 9. partial to 10. vivid **K.** 1. c 2. b 3. d 4. a 5. a **L.** a. 7 b. 2 c. 3 d. 10 e. 4 f. 9 g. 5 h. 8 i. 6 **M.** 1. d 2. d 3. c. 4. c 5. a **N.** 1. dilapidated 2. enterprising 3. Proponents 4. nickname 5. is banned 6. substantial 7. duplicated 8. lingered 9. merely 10. replica **Q.** 1. a. frustrating b. Frustrated c. frustration d. has frustrated 2. a. exaggeration b. to exaggerate c. exaggerated 3. a. inspiration b. inspired c. have inspired d. inspiring 4. a. industrialized b. industries c. industrial d. industrious 5. a. conversational b. conversationalist c. conversed d. conversation 6. a. comfortable b. comfortably c. comforting d. comforted e. comfort 7. a. appropriately b. inappropriate c. appropriateness 8. a. distinguish b. Distinguished c. distinguishing 9. a. traditional b. tradition c. traditionally 10. a. described b. descriptive c. description d. descriptively **R.** 6. Pilgrims

Chapter 2:

C. 1. T 2. F 3. F 4. F 5. F 6. T 7. F 8. T 9. T 10. F **D.** 1. by 2. from 3. for 4. by 5. by 6. to 7. under 8. of 9. On 10. for 11. by 12. to 13. along/on 14. for 15. with **E.** 1. spectacular 2. to spot 3. masterpiece 4. covertly 5. oblivious to 6. pity 7. are launched 8. worshipers 9. multitude 10. conforming to **K.** 1. c 2. d 3. a 4. c 5. d **L.** a. 7 b. 4 c. 9 d. 5 e. 8 f. 1 g. 6 **M.** 1. a 2. c 3. c 4. d 5. b **N.** 1. was postponed 2. extensive 3. controversial 4. remote 5. outcome 6. were evacuated 7. potentially 8. resemble 9. was spoiled 10. risky **Q.** 1. a. associates b. association c. associated 2. a. despite b. in spite 3. a. relies b. reliance c. reliant d. reliable e. reliability 4. a. opposition b. opponents c. oppose d. opposing e. opposed 5. a. spectacular b. spectacle c. spectacularly d. Spectators 6. a. controversy b. controversial 7. a. disposal b. dispose c. disposable 8. a. pollution b. polluter c. pollutants d. pollutes e. Polluted

9. a. attracts b. attractions c. attractive d. attractively 10. a. to conform
b. Conformity c. non-conformist

Chapter 3:

C. 1. F 2. T 3. T 4. F 5. F 6. T 7. F 8. T 9. F 10. F **D.** 1. a 2. X/a
3. the 4. an 5. X 6. the 7. a 8. X 9. X 10. an 11. the 12. the
E. 1. was incapacitated 2. Supposedly 3. stereotype 4. conveniences 5. sobering
6. reward 7. fatalistic 8. take time off 9. room for improvement 10. accomplished **K.** 1. e 2. b 3. a 4. c 5. c **L.** a. 5 b. 3 c. 7 d. 4 e. 8
M. 1. b 2. c 3. c. 4. a 5. b 6. c **N.** 1. lucrative 2. consumption 3. to cut
down on 4. symptoms 5. to quit 6. Drowsiness 7. advocate 8. unaware of
9. link 10. challenge **Q.** 1. a. irritates b. irritating c. irritation d. irritable
2. a. consumption b. consume c. consumers 3. a. withdrew b. withdrawal
c. withdrawn 4. a. convenience b. inconvenient c. conveniently 5. a. reside
b. residents c. residential d. residences 6. a. Beware b. aware c. awareness
d. unaware 7. a. Formal b. formally c. formerly d. former 8. a. significant
b. significantly c. significance d. signified 9. a. recognized b. recognized
c. recognition d. recognizable 10. a. invented b. invention c. inventor
d. inventive

Chapter 4:

C. 1. T 2. F 3. F 4. T 5. F 6. T 7. F 8. F 9. F 10. T **D.** 1. in
2. from 3. to 4. for 5. of 6. with 7. for 8. during/in 9. of 10. from 11. for
12. to 13. in 14. to 15. to 16. Of 17. of 18. for 19. in **E.** 1. opted
2. stretch 3. hovered 4. impact 5. in short 6. trim 7. predictable 8. impostor 9. adequately 10. valid **K.** 1. b 2. b 3. d 4. e 5. c. **L.** a. 5 b. 8
c. 4 d. 2 e. 7 f. 3 g. 6 **M.** 1. c 2. a 3. b 4. b 5. a **N.** 1. segregated
2. rare 3. preached 4. discrimination 5. struggle 6. discrepancy 7. are barred
8. ineligible 9. contaminates 10. persisted **Q.** 1. a. Illegally b. illegal
c. illegality d. to legalize 2. a. ambitious b. ambitiously c. ambition
3. a. resist b. irresistable c. resistant d. resistance 4. a. discrimination
b. discriminates c. discriminatory 5. a. persistence b. persistent c. persisted
d. persistently 6. a. Contamination b. Contaminated c. contaminate
d. Contaminants 7. a. valid b. invalid c. validity d. validated 8. a. fantastic
b. fantastically c. fantasized d. fantasy 9. a. amusement b. have amused
c. amusing d. amused 10. a. specified b. specifically c. specific
d. specifications

Chapter 5:

C. 1. T 2. T 3. F 4. T 5. F 6. F 7. T 8. F 9. F 10. T **D.** 1. an 2. X
3. the 4. X 5. the 6. the 7. an 8. the 9. the 10. a 11. X 12. X 13. a
14. the 15. an 16. a 17. a **E.** 1. abrupt 2. to exploit 3. virtually 4. circumstances 5. prosperity 6. intact 7. had sworn 8. fan 9. quaint 10. heyday
K. 1. e 2. d 3. a 4. b 5. c **L.** a. 10 b. 7 c. 3 d. 11 e. 5 f. 6 g. 9
M. 1. d 2. a 3. b 4. d 5. c **N.** 1. traits 2. innovations 3. devastating
4. depleted 5. remarkable 6. to keep up with 7. has sustained 8. compensated
9. replenished 10. defects **Q.** 1. a. prospered b. prosperity c. prosperous
2. a. products b. production c. produces d. productivity e. productively
f. productive 3. a. compensation b. are compensated 4. a. depletion b. To deplete 5. a. were devastated b. devastating c. devastation d. devastated
6. a. tasty b. tasted c. tasteless d. tastefully e. Tasteful f. taste
7. a. progress b. progressively c. progress d. progression e. progressive
8. a. substantial b. Substances c. substantiates d. substantially 9. a. remark
b. remark c. remarkable d. remarkably 10. a. was charmed b. charmingly
c. charming d. charm

Chapter 6:

C. 1. F 2. T 3. T 4. F 5. T 6. F 7. F 8. F 9. T 10. F **D.** 1. In 2. on 3. of 4. of 5. during 6. of 7. of 8. in 9. In 10. with 11. for 12. of 13. to 14. of 15. to 16. for 17. for **E.** 1. crippled 2. barren 3. automated 4. congested 5. vastness 6. had the upper hand 7. to picture 8. suffocating 9. All kidding aside 10. coincidence **K.** 1. c 2. a 3. a 4. b 5. c 6. c **L.** a. 6 b. 3 c. 7 d. 9 e. 5 **M.** 1. c 2. d 3. a 4. c 5. a 6. a **N.** 1. plight 2. were propelled 3. Initially 4. portray 5. Despair 6. fostered 7. self-esteem 8. hostile 9. harsh 10. ambivalent **Q.** 1. a. intolerable b. tolerance c. tolerate d. Intolerant 2. a. Automation b. automated c. to automate 3. a. ambivalent b. ambivalence 4. a. to predict b. predictions c. unpredictable d. unpredictability e. predictable 5. a. Competitive b. competed c. Competition 6. a. portray b. portrayal c. portrait 7. a. propellers b. propelled 8. a. ignored b. ignorant c. ignorance 9. a. conflict b. conflict c. conflicting 10. a. impression b. are impressed c. impressive

Chapter 7:

C. 1. F 2. T 3. F 4. F 5. T 6. T 7. F 8. F 9. F 10. T **D.** 1. a 2. the 3. the 4. the 5. the 6. the 7. the 8. X 9. the 10. an 11. X 12. the 13. the 14. a 15. the 16. X 17. the 18. a 19. X 20. the **E.** 1. otherwise 2. a change of pace 3. boast of 4. as far as I can see 5. mutual 6. merits 7. to make a detour 8. was founded 9. landscape 10. stuck out like a sore thumb **K.** 1. b 2. a and c 3. a 4. c 5. d **L.** a. 6 b. 8 c. 3 d. 2 e. 7 **M.** 1. c 2. b 3. c 4. c 5. a 6. b 7. b **N.** 1. faced 2. ran out of 3. abundance 4. mighty 5. sacrificed 6. shortage 7. compromise 8. have survived 9. dwindled 10. to take for granted **Q.** 1. a. resentful b. resented c. resentment d. resentfully 2. a. survive b. survivors c. surviving d. survival 3. a. decided b. decision c. decisively d. decisive 4. a. has fascinated b. fascinating c. Fascinated d. fascination 5. a. basically b. basis c. is based d. basic 6. a. imagination b. imagine c. imaginative d. imaginary 7. a. relatively b. relationship, relates c. relative 8. a. necessary b. necessitates c. necessarily d. necessity 9. a. to compare b. comparable c. comparatively d. comparison 10. a. hard b. hard c. hardened d. hardly

Chapter 8:

C. 1. T 2. F 3. T 4. F 5. F 6. F 7. F 8. F 9. T 10. T **D.** 1. During 2. in 3. between 4. of 5. at 6. to 7. for 8. through/in 9. of 10. of 11. with 12. of 13. for 14. of 15. in 16. of 17. on/along 18. through/in 19. between 20. of 21. of **E.** 1. literally 2. plagued 3. was spared 4. highlights 5. has retained 6. haven 7. imposing 8. fragrant 9. being persecuted 10. have carved **K.** 1. b 2. c 3. d 4. d 5. c **L.** a. 10 b. 2 c. 6 d. 1 e. 8 f. 4 **M.** 1. c 2. a 3. b 4. d 5. c **N.** 1. accessible 2. to bear in mind 3. awesome 4. dilemma 5. outstanding 6. peered 7. flock 8. ensures 9. unintentionally 10. followed suit **Q.** 1. a. isolation b. isolates c. isolated 2. a. enthusiasts b. enthusiasm c. enthusiastic d. enthusiastically 3. a. variety b. various c. varies 4. a. are considering b. considerable c. considerably d. consideration e. Considering f. considerate 5. a. intention b. unintentionally c. intend d. intentional 6. a. restrictive b. restrictions c. restricted d. restrict 7. a. proposal b. proposed c. proposed 8. a. appreciation b. to appreciate c. appreciative 9. a. originated b. Originally c. origin d. original 10. a. creation b. created c. creative d. creatively e. creativity

Chapter 9:

C. 1. F 2. T 3. T 4. F 5. T 6. F 7. T 8. F 9. T 10. F **D.** 1. a 2. the 3. a 4. X 5. The 6. a 7. the 8. the 9. the 10. X 11. the 12. a 13. the

14. the   15. an   **E.** 1. barely   2. petrified   3. monstrous   4. bet   5. elaborate
6. in a row   7. no wonder   8. to top it off   9. to steer it   10. supportive   **K.** 1. b
2. c   3. e   4. e   5. c   **L.** a. 4 b. 5 c. 2 d. 3 e. 6   **M.** 1. b 2. b 3. b 4. a
5. c   6. b   7. c   **N.** 1. was engulfed   2. drifted   3. abrasive   4. core   5. long-
awaited   6. collided   7. determined   8. casualties   9. anticipate   10. debris
Q. 1.   a. anticipated   b. anticipation   c. anticipate   2. a. evasive   b. evasion
c. evaded   3. a. protects   b. protection   c. protective   d. protector
4. a. determined   b. determined   c. determination   5. a. agreement   b. agreeably
c. agreed   d. agreeable   6. a. collided   b. collision   7. a. capable   b. capability
c. capably   8. a. expressionless   b. expressed   c. expression   d. expressive
9. a. appearance   b. appeared   c. apparently   d. apparent   10. a. theorize
b. theoretical   c. theory   d. Theoretically

Chapter 10:
   C. 1. F 2. T 3. F 4. F 5. T 6. T 7. F 8. F 9. F 10. T   **D.** 1. off 2. of
3. In   4. in   5. of   6. to   7. with   8. in/during   9. of   10. for   11. under   12. in
13. in   14. from   15. of   16. to   17. for   18. of   19. with   20. to   21. for   22. between   23. with   24. to   **E.** 1. bonus   2. off-limits   3. out of this world   4. harbors 5. are conducive to 6. drawback 7. wholeheartedly 8. repertoire 9. altruistic 10. was mellowed   **K.** 1. b 2. c 3. d 4. d 5. b   **L.** a. 4 b. 8 c. 3 d. 2
e. 6 f. 5   **M.** 1. b 2. c 3. b 4. a 5. d   **N.** 1. encroaching 2. disregard
3. indiscriminately   4. stringent   5. lull   6. revival   7. drastic   8. absurd
9. eradication   10. roam   **Q.** 1.   a. reluctant   b. reluctantly   c. reluctance
2. a. diverse   b. diversity   c. to diversify   3. a. optimism   b. optimistic   c. opti-
mists   d. optimistically   4. a. serene   b. serenely   c. serenity   5. a. expected
b. expectantly   c. expectant   d. expectations   6.   a. to impose   b. imposition
c. imposing   7.   a. expendable   b. expenses   c. expensive   d. expend
8. a. rarely   b. rare   c. rarity   9.   a. excellence   b. excellently   c. excel
d. excellent   10.   a. symbol b. symbolic c. symbolize d. symbolically